UNDERSTANDING
PERVERSION
IN CLINICAL PRACTICE

The Society of Analytical Psychology Monograph Series
Hazel Robinson (Series Editor)
Published and distributed by Karnac Books

Other titles in the SAP Monograph Series

Understanding Narcissism in Clinical Practice
Hazel Robinson & Victoria Graham Fuller

Orders
Tel: +44 (0)20 8969 4454; Fax: +44 (0)20 8969 5585
Email: shop@karnacbooks.com
www.karnacbooks.com

UNDERSTANDING PERVERSION IN CLINICAL PRACTICE

Structure and Strategy in the Psyche

Fiona Ross

LONDON   NEW YORK

First published in 2003 by
H. Karnac (Books) Ltd.
6 Pembroke Buildings, London NW10 6RE

British Library Cataloguing in Publication Data

A C.I.P. for this book is available from the British Library

ISBN 185575 9330

Edited, designed, and produced by Cortex Publishing

Printed in Great Britain

www.karnacbooks.com

CONTENTS

About the Author   ix

Preface to the Series   xi

Introduction   1

CHAPTER ONE

   The Character of Perversion   5
      Definitions
      Characteristics of Perversion

CHAPTER TWO
   Deception   19
      Ms S
      The Parts and the Whole
      Attacks on Linking
      Deception and Defence
      Criminality

v

CHAPTER THREE
The Trickster   33
Mr A
Narcissism and Excitement
without Reflection
Attachment
The Body
Mr E

CHAPTER FOUR

Female Perversion   47
Male and Female
Women and Criminality
Repetition
Mothering
Jane

CHAPTER FIVE

Assessment   59
The Operation of a Perverse Structure
The Extent to which Perverse Qualities
are Erotic
The Extent of Aggression, Sadism and
Violence in Life, Fantasies and Dreams
The Pervasiveness of Perversity
and its Lifestyle Dominance
The Patient's Awareness of his own Perverse
Qualities
The Patient's Ability and Motivation for
Change

CHAPTER SIX
The Psychotherapeutic Relationship   69
Aims
The Therapeutic Alliance and Defences
Mr Y
The Inner Child
Action, Acting and Acting Out
Interpreting Negative Feelings
The Body
Deceptive and Perverse Qualities
in the Psychotherapist
Self Respect and Self Management

References   83

Index   89

ABOUT THE AUTHOR

Fiona Ross is a Jungian analyst and professional member of the Society of Analytical Psychology. She works in a private practice in South London and teaches at the SAP and other training institutions. She has contributed a chapter to *Contemporary Jungian Analysis* (1998, ed. Alister and Hauke, Routledge). Her MA thesis was on the 'Internalised Victim-Perpetrator Relationship' in survivors of child sexual abuse. She is also an Educational Psychologist and an Associate Fellow of the British Psychological Society.

PREFACE TO THE SERIES

This series of clinical practice monographs is being produced primarily for the benefit of trainees on psychotherapy and psychodynamic counselling courses. The authors are Jungian analysts who have trained at the Society of Analytical Psychology, with extensive experience of teaching both theory and practice.

The rationale for this series is in part to do with the expensive and time-consuming task of accessing all the pertinent books and papers for any one clinical subject. These single-issue monographs have been kept relatively brief and cannot claim to be comprehensive, but we hope that each volume brings together some of the major theorists and their ideas in a comprehensible way, including references to significant and interesting texts.

Much of the literature provided for students of psychotherapy has been generated from four or five-times weekly analytic work, which can be confusing for students whose psychodynamic courses may be structured on the basis of less frequent sessions. The authors of these monographs have aimed to hold this difference in mind. A decision was taken to maintain the terms 'therapist' and 'patient' throughout, although the clinical work referred to ranges from once weekly to five-times weekly. We have also borrowed shamelessly from the work of our supervisees in many settings, for which we thank them. We are even more indebted to our patients. Where a patient's material is recognisable, their permission to publish has been given. In other cases, we have amalgamated and disguised clinical material to preserve anonymity.

When a training is 'eclectic', that is, offering several different psychodynamic perspectives, a particular difficulty can arise with the integration – or rather *non*-integration of psychoanalytic and Jungian analytic ideas. The teaching on such trainings is often presented in blocks: a term devoted to 'Freud', another to 'Jung' and so on. It is frequently the students who are left with the job of trying to see where these do and do not fit together, and this can be a daunting, even depressing experience. SAP analysts are in a better position than most to offer some help here, because its members have been working on this integration since the organisation was founded in 1946. Although retaining a strong relationship with 'Zurich' or 'Classical' Jungian scholarship, SAP members have evolved equally strong links with psychoanalysis. Recent years have brought a number of joint conferences to supplement the many individual 'cross-party' alliances.

Any patient, but particularly a trainee, will naturally tend to adopt the language of his or her therapist when talking about their work. Those readers who are unfamiliar with Jungian terms may wish to consult the *Critical Dictionary of Jungian Analysis* (Samuels, Plaut & Shorter, 1986), whilst those unfamiliar with psychoanalytic terms may turn to *The Language of Psychoanalysis* (Laplanche & Pontalis, 1988). Strangely though, all patients are united by their human suffering far more than they are divided by language. Just as people from non-Western cultures have to make what they can of their western-trained psychotherapists, so each patient-therapist pair eventually evolve a unique way of understanding their joint experiences in the consulting-room. It is our view that each stream of psychotherapy has strengths and weaknesses, and the wise trainee will take the best bits from each. We hope that this series may help a little with the psychodynamic 'Tower of Babel'.

We want to thank Karnac Books for their patience and help in bringing the series to publication. Our intention is to add to the series of monographs each year, gradually building up a 'stable' of texts on the principle clinical issues. I therefore want to end by thanking my colleagues within the SAP for their work so far – and for their work to come.

Hazel Robinson
Series Editor

INTRODUCTION

The trouble with a concept is that you have it all there, in a nutshell. Perversion as a concept is a hard nut to crack. If it stays in its shell, it becomes a specialist subject; a particular area of expertise that only a few people know about and others should not meddle with. The behaviour lurking under the perversion umbrella then becomes seen as different from what 'normal' people do, sometimes different enough to define a person's identity as a 'pervert'.

This monograph is intended to be a hammer to crack the shell and let bits of nut fly out in different directions. It will look at the nature of the perverse relationship

    a)   as the patient presents himself and his significant others in psychotherapy

    b)   as it is experienced in the therapeutic relationship between psychotherapist and patient

    c)   as a (sometimes useful) potential of the psyche in people who would not be considered sexually perverse, including psychotherapists.

The third area is of great importance, as one of the main difficulties of working with perversion is the strength of the countertransference. By this I mean the psychotherapist's emotional attitude towards the patient. As with all pathologies, emotional understanding of the patient comes through the psychotherapist finding within himself or herself some of the qualities experienced as belonging to the patient. If the patient comes with symptoms of anxiety it is not difficult to identify with this. If the patient's difficulties are obsessional or compulsive, again the psychotherapist may well be able to locate and acknowledge something similar in his or her own psyche. In both cases the patient's difficulties might lead the psychotherapist to feel empathy and sympathy for the patient: it is easy to feel sympathetic towards someone whose symptoms are likely to cause more difficulty to themselves than to others. What happens, though, if the compulsive patient takes on a compulsion to burgle? Here our capacity for empathy may undergo a shift; we may feel greater identification with the occupants of the houses who have suffered intrusion and loss. If we take a further step in this direction and consider a patient whose compulsions are not directed at the symbolic house/body but involve predatory encroachment on real bodies, our countertransference reactions may well be those of outrage, disgust, fear etc. - reactions of the imagined victim. We may then have set up an internal oppositional relationship in which we attribute to the perpetrator/patient all the negative qualities we do not associate with either the victim or with ourselves.

The monograph explores perversion as a structural organisation of the psyche that people can move in and out of with varying degrees of flexibility. Some people find their own psychic structure rigid and implacably resistant to reconstitution, to the extent that it governs their personality. The repetitive and compulsive strategies typical of perversion result from just such an inflexible psychic structure.

There are six chapters. The first chapter looks at the combination of characteristics that come together to form the particular character of perversion, which can then be compared with, and distinguished from, other types of psychopathology. The next chapter explores the importance of an understanding of deception, not only to comprehend the difficulties of the perverse patient, but in the understanding of all unconscious processes. The Trickster is the subject of the third chapter. This Jungian archetypal figure comes from the deepest layer of the unconscious, with deceptive qualities that permeate every level of the psyche. Female perversion deserves a chapter of its own since the manifestation of perversion in women is so closely related to the female body with its reproductive functions, and to motherhood. The chapter on assessment addresses the difficulties of the initial encounter with the perverse patient, whose pathology may feel quite inaccessible, disconnected from his outer presentation and even contradictory to his own description of himself and his need for psychotherapy. The final chapter looks at perversion as a quality of the relationship between patient and psychotherapist and also as a tendency within the psychotherapist's own psyche.

Some terminology needs clarification. Sometimes I write of 'perversion' or 'perverse strategies' but I also use terms such as 'the perverse patient'. Using the term 'perverse' adjectivally is not intended to mean that the perversity is permanently attached to the patient. It is used for ease of communication to describe the way in which the patient, or part of the patient's psyche, is functioning at a particular time or in a particular context.

I have used the pronoun 'he' for the patient. This is principally because most of the writing about sexual perversion has been by men writing about men. To complement this the psychotherapist is referred to as 'she'.

I am not aiming to pathologise those who have made sexual choices with partners and have a reciprocal relationship that is not essentially destructive to either party. Many homosexual relationships could be described in this way. Freud did not regard homosexuality as a perversion, but an inversion: a term he applied to deviation in the sexual object. Perversion was a deviation in the sexual aim. For him, this was a deviation from copulative, non-incestuous heterosexuality.

I have treated homosexual patients and have found it rare for such patients to come into therapy through concern about their sexual orientation per se. More often the doubt arises through secondary problems that make patients feel that life would have been a great deal easier if they had felt free to make heterosexual object choices.

Finally, I have found the issue of presenting case material difficult. Patients who have problems associated with perverse functioning have often had experiences of abuse and of other people taking advantage of them. They may have low self-esteem and may feel deeply ashamed to be the people they are doing the things that they do. I have therefore only used undisguised clinical material in cases where I have felt that it would not be too conflictual for the patient to be asked for consent. Other case material has had identifying features removed or altered to protect the patient's anonymity.

CHAPTER ONE

The Character of Perversion

Psychotherapy is about 'the space between'. It is not just about the patient and certainly not just about the psychotherapist but it is about what happens between them. But psychotherapy focuses on another space between that is particularly important in the treatment of the perverse patient. This second space is between what the patient actually does and his experience. The first space is *inter*psychic and is crossed backwards and forwards again and again, by interactions between the couple in the consulting room. The second is an *intra*psychic space and the dark hiding place of meaning.

It can be extremely difficult to understand the connection between the perverse behavioural symptomatology described by a patient in his relationships with others and the typically charming exterior and the engaging manner he initially displays towards his psychotherapist.

It might be useful to think of patients driving to psychotherapy in their own vehicle. We would easily recognise those with bumps and scratches inflicted through their trafficking in the world and with a little more skill we would diagnose a bent axle or a cracked chassis. It is not so unusual for a new patient to drive to therapy in a heavily armoured tank. We see the armour-plating and know there is a long hard battle ahead but at least we have sight of what we, and the patient, are up against. When the perverse patient comes, he comes in his submarine and the only part he allows into the consulting room is the periscope. This periscope is alert, responsive and adept at engagement, so we may feel optimistic about forming a good therapeutic alliance. The trouble is that we will have engaged with a part that does not represent the whole. In fact the periscope is nothing like the submarine. Usually periscopes communicate with their submarines through an arrangement of carefully placed mirrors. In the case of the perverse person there is a complicated system of distorting mirrors designed to misinform and to deceive. The deception is not only endemic to the internal system but also designed to confuse communications between the inner and the outer world.

Definitions

Louise Kaplan usefully describes a perversion as a mental or psychological strategy. The aim of the strategy is to deceive and to mislead (Kaplan 1991:9). Chapter 2 will expand on this essentially deceptive quality of perversion that confuses the onlooker as to the underlying meaning of behaviour. On the surface there might appear to be something neat and recognisable about perversions. This is particularly so because they are behavioural and can be classified.

The Diagnostic and Statistical Manual of Mental Disorders, 4th Edition (American Psychiatric Association, 1994) classifies perversions according to their specific behavioural manifestations. Here they are named Paraphilias (para = deviant, philia = attraction). Below are those listed with my own brief summary of characteristics. Readers are advised to consult DSM-IV for a definitive psychiatric description:

Exhibitionism: exposure of the genitals to a stranger, with or without masturbation, usually with the conscious desire to shock or sexually arouse the other.

Fetishism: sexual interest in nonliving objects, commonly women's clothing, particularly underwear and footwear. Tactile or sensory contact (e.g. smelling) with the object or use of the object by a sexual partner may be necessary for sexual satisfaction.

Frotteurism: rubbing the genital against a non-consenting person, usually in a crowded place. Also fondling of a woman's genitals or breasts.

Paedophilia: sexual activity, with or without intercourse, with a pre-pubescent child.

Sexual Masochism: acts that involve suffering or humiliation perpetrated either by oneself or a sexual partner. They include bondage, whipping, cutting, sexual servitude, oxygen deprivation (hypoxyphilia).

Sexual Sadism: deriving sexual satisfaction from the psychological or physical suffering of the other.

Transvestic Fetishism: sexual excitement through cross-dressing, usually with masturbation.

Voyeurism: secretly watching people undressing, naked, or engaged in sexual activity.

Examples of Paraphilias Not Categorised: telephone scatologia (obscene phone calls), necrophilia (corpses), partialism (exclusive focus on part of body), zoophilia (animals), coprophilia (sexual arousal dependant on excremental activity of some sort) klismaphilia (enemas), and urophilia (urine).

Specific expressions of perverse desire may change with the evolution of society. Stalking, for example, is now regarded as a dangerous infringement of individual rights and could be categorised as a perversion. Development in technology has opened up new channels for the communication of pornographic material, and for the seduction of minors through internet chat rooms.

Perhaps there is only one underlying perversion, which expresses itself in a variety of behavioural outcomes. If that were so, we would be looking at a syndrome or cluster of characteristics indicating a particular organisation of psychic structure, protected by a defensive system. We could begin to understand this structure and its defences by looking at some of the characteristic themes associated with sexually perverse acts. Sandwiching the word 'perversion' between 'sexually' and 'acts' suggests a comprehensive model linking the instinctual, the emotional and the behavioural. I will present the characteristic themes which appear within a perverse system and then return to them individually and in combination showing how the system is established and how it functions to preserve the integrity of the self.

Characteristics of Perversion

Anxiety is a bubbling undercurrent lapping at ego weaknesses and at other vulnerable structures in the troubled psyche. If perversion has taken over, the anxiety ceases to express itself through communicable neurotic symptoms that the psychotherapist might receive as the patient's way of showing distress and asking for help. When the rigidity of a perverse solution cuts in, the patient's presentation of his difficulties can seem strange, different, encapsulated, inaccessible and often meaningless. Connected with anxiety is the **psychic conflict**, which becomes *embodied* and is expressed in **acting out**. The threat to psychic equilibrium leads to a compulsion to act as a substitute for the internal processes of remembering and reflecting. If the patient cannot bear to remember or to reflect, the only way to resurrect deeply disturbing material may be to act out. At least this gives an indication of the distress the patient suffers even if the acting out may itself be destructive or retaliatory. In the case of perversion, acting out usually involves a crossing of the body barrier: it is an intrusive relationship with the body of another person. When the patient is in a heightened state of anxiety, perverse acting out can restore a feeling of self-esteem. Bodily action becomes the psychic regulator. There is a compulsion to alleviate anxiety by distracting the psyche so it focuses on short-term goals that offer excitement and relief.

In the perverse act there is a **denial of difference**. There is a denial of generally accepted boundaries of age, position, part/whole, and of opposites. This is an undifferentiated world of psychic shit (Chasseguet-Smirgel 1985:128).

The Core Complex is at the heart of perversion. (Glasser 1979:278). This is the addictive push-pull movement of attraction-repulsion: a craving for closeness or merger with the loved object, which, when acted upon, leads to an experience of terror at being overwhelmed or devoured. Although present in other pathologies, in sexual perversion the intense feelings, including aggression, have become *eroticised*.

Splitting and part-object relating characterise a world of fantasy imposed upon an unwilling other. There is little sense of the wholeness of a two-person relationship. (Stoller 1986:x) refers to the dehumanised, unloving aspects of human behaviour that emphasise anatomical more than interpersonal gratification.

Idealisation of part objects and idealisation of the pre-pubescent self. The well-known figure of Peter Pan could be seen as J. M. Barrie's idealised pre-pubescent image of himself. **Pre-genital sexuality** in perverse adults results from a fixation at a premature stage of psychosexual development rather than regression from full genital sexuality to an earlier stage.

Humiliation and Retaliatory Triumph. The perverse act is characterised by overwhelming hostility and aggression. Some understanding of the retaliatory dynamic may be found in the tragic case of the paedophilic murder of a nine-year-old boy some years ago. When previously in Wormwood Scrubs, one of the killers, Timothy Morss, had attended group therapy sessions for sex offenders. In one such session he outlined his favourite fantasy. He wanted to "pluck a blond boy, aged between eight and thirteen, from the street, take him somewhere quiet, bugger him, strangle him and then dispose of his body". (Campbell, Elliott and Bowcott 1996:6) This was a man who had himself been sexually abused as a child. It has the quality of reversal of opposites - the humiliated child becomes the persecuting adult.

How do these themes come together in perversion? For Stoller perverse behaviour is that which seeks to harm or dehumanise (Stoller 1986:211-12). McDougall defines perverse acts as those "in which an individual (1) imposes personal wishes and conditions on someone who does not wish to be included in the perverse individual's sexual scenario (as in the case of rape, voyeurism, and exhibitionism); or (2) seduces a non-responsible individual (such as a child or a mentally disturbed adult)" (McDougall 1995: 177). According to Cassell's English Dictionary perversion is "The act of perverting; a misinterpretation, misapplication, or corruption; the act of forsaking one's religion; sexual derangement." This suggests cognitive, behavioural, spiritual and sexual aspects to perversion. There is a strong sense of wrongness in this definition: a moral or even legal wrongness. How do we understand this wrongness in psychoanalytic terms? The most useful concept I have found to contain this and other facets of perversion is that of deception. This will be the focus of Chapter 2.

Returning to the characteristics of perversion and their interrelationship, **anxiety** heads the list. Because it is an 'undercurrent' in the unconscious, it is also a driving force that moves the ego to action. The intensity of the anxiety is so severe that there is a call for an immediate solution to alleviate the suffering of the self. This anxiety fuels a perverse syndrome of addiction and somatisation with risk taking and sometimes criminal behaviour in the outer world. The perverse act allows the patient to escape temporarily from his anxiety and therefore from the need for further perverse action until the level of anxiety begins to rise again. So the patient may appear to be presenting with an episodic disturbance, whereas he could more usefully be seen as taken up by a perverse cycle in which anxiety builds to a critical point and is then dispelled by action. The cycle affords immediate, but short term, protection from the experience of deep depressive anxieties and grave feelings of loss. The action circumvents conflict in that the anxiety does not lead the patient into contemplation of his inner world but turns outwards and drives the ego to act. The experience of anxiety is so unbearable that the patient turns away from his inner world to find an immediate solution to the suffering of the self. It is this urgency that causes the ego to become linked to action rather than neurosis, although it does not in itself explain why such action is perverse.

Not only is the individual locked within an endless cycle but he is also fixated at an earlier stage of development. For Freud all sexual aberration resulted from fixations and traumas in childhood. Jung might have associated such behaviour with fixation on an **extroverted attitude** without inner reflection or an adjustment only to the demands of the external. "An individual who adjusts himself to it is admittedly conforming to the style of his environment, but together with his whole surrounding he is in an abnormal situation with respect to the universally valid laws of life" (Jung 1963:335).

Here Jung is describing a drivenness, a need to find a solution in the outer world even if this upsets the balance of the psyche and deprives the inner world of the ability to reflect and find inner meaning in outer action. So preoccupying and obsessive is this solution finding in

perverse behaviour that many men placed in Grendon
Prison for sex offences against children saw sex offending
as their true occupation rather than their stated job or
profession. This preoccupation with behaviour confirms the
extent to which, in the psychic sense, perversion is about
staying still and not about development and change. Freud
described the work of psychoanalysis as "Remembering,
repeating and working through" (Freud 1924:147). This he
considered to be the opposite of acting out, in which the
patient avoids remembering anything that is forgotten or
repressed but alternatively acts it out from his unconscious.
The patient repeats without knowing. This dismissal of
the value of acting out was challenged by Greenacre, who
described acting out as a form of remembering rather than
its opposite (Greenacre 1950). Limentani distinguished
three fairly well defined groups of acting out: 1. Acting out
as an expression of the individual's fantasy life. This may
lead to an act which is difficult to understand but can be
understood if the motivation is allowed into consciousness.
2. Acting out geared to finding a solution to internal conflicts.
Limentani sees this type of behaviour disorder as oedipal
in origin and as typical of many sexual offenders and of
cases of compulsive taking and driving away. 3. Acting out
as a form of communication with the analyst (including
messages that the patient wishes to solve his psychic
conflicts through anti-social behaviour). All three types of
behaviour are within the range of a patient who frequently
resorts to perverse solutions (Limentani 1966:74).

Acting out always involves **denial**. It denies the
expression of parts of the self, which might allow for
reflection and it denies the experience of psychic pain by
diversionary behaviour. Chasseguet-Smirgel goes much
further in describing the omnipotence of this denial as
almost a total denial of reality. "It is a fatherless universe
submitted to the total abolition of the limits between the
objects and even between the molecules, a universe which
has become totally malleable, a fatherless universe where

the subject confers upon himself the creator's powers, the subjects having abolished all genital procreation in favour of anal production" (Chasseguet-Smirgel 1985:122).

Such denial is a turning away from reality testing. Klein describes the developmental importance of reality testing in seeing that internal objects are safe by good experiences with outer objects. Inner reality is tested by outer reality. With every positive experience the child's good inner objects become more firmly established. When the depressive position arises, the ego is forced to develop methods of defence, including manic defences that are essentially directed against the 'pining' for the loved object (Klein 1975:344).

In perversion the denial involves a distortion of what is whole and separate, what is different and the same. There is a oneness of process and content that Jung might see as a return to the mentality of participation mystique; a reliving of the infantile non-differentiation of subject and object as well as a return to the primordial unconscious state (Jung 1946:305). Denial is often associated with violent trauma. An assault on the developing psyche can lead to a state in which the opposing internal pairs, or syzygies, (good/bad, victim/victimiser and pleasure/pain) are no longer consciously discriminated but are highly charged, resulting in continuous unconscious oscillation between extremes. Simultaneous experiences by a child of love and abuse from the same person may accentuate the perverse character of the trauma and increase the risk of the victim's identification with the aggressor. There is an abolition of difference particularly of opposites. It is a world of fantasy in which one person's fantasies are imposed upon another.

Perversion is a triumphant act. The man has displayed his masculine prowess and dominance but he has also exposed the opposite aspect of himself, the humiliated, helpless, persecuted child. Internally the conquering hero has had his revenge by defeating the unbearable feelings of anxiety and humiliation. Confusingly, the masculine hero is also angry at what his false solution forces him to do, which is to kill off the passive, submissive female he would also like to be. Unbearable psychic conflict has forced him to make an unconscious choice and he has come down on the side of the seemingly strong. By doing so he has fallen into his shadow. The choice has forced out the other, freer self. To quell its appetite, he has fed his frightened child self to the ferocious dragon he has become. In so doing he is caught up in an addictive and hopeless cycle. The lack of opposition to the imposing psychic structure is associated with the elimination of the transcendent function that represents a linkage between real and imaginary, or rational and irrational data, thus bridging the gulf between consciousness and the unconscious. The transcendent function "is a natural process, a manifestation of the energy that springs from the tension of opposites" (Jung 1916:79). It expresses itself through symbols and it facilitates a transition from one psychological attitude or condition to another. It can only operate on opposing forces presenting a certain degree of differentiation. Only when these forces are considered and discriminated and when the painful tension between them is endured as consciously as possible may a symbol emerge from the conflict, inaugurating new possibilities. Without this, the furious attempts of the crushed child to remove himself from his experience may result in a solution tainted with destructiveness. Abuse and trauma attack symbol-forming capacity and move the possibilities of true transformation into the concrete world and into the body. Symbols act as transformers, they function to convert libido to a higher form.

Edinger uses alchemical imagery in describing the individual as a vessel that must act as a container to hold the opposites in balance. "The ego keeps its integrity only if it does not identify with one of the opposites and if it understands how to hold the balance between them. This remains possible only if it remains conscious of both at once" (Edinger 1994:15). With a perverse psychic structure the ego and self no longer feed each other and the wounded self drives the ego in love and hate from an urge to annihilate combined with a desire to re-establish unity.

This psychic conflict is central to the **Core Complex**. Glasser thought of perversion as a complex of elements arranged to make up the large perversion molecule. In the centre of the molecule is an expression of a deep longing for a coming together, and being at one, with the object. There is a wish to return to the close symbiotic relationship with the mother (Glasser 1979:278). The perverse person differs from others in that if he becomes at one with the object, the longing disappears but the closeness is associated with over-whelming fear of engulfment and annihilation, leading to a desire to get away emotionally, intellectually and physically. This narcissistic withdrawal is accompanied by feelings of isolation, deprivation and lack of self-esteem, fuelling an intense need to get back to the object and eradicate anxiety, so the circular movement repeats itself. There is a push/pull experience that drives the patient into hopeless feelings of being driven and of loss of self. In sexually perverse patients the Core Complex is characterised by association with sexuality and excitement. The push-pull feeling is experienced as powerful, dangerous and erotic.

Jungian psychology describes the regressive desire to return to oneness with the mother as an innate incestuous desire. The collective unconscious is the mother of the psyche and the ego will be lost, overwhelmed or annihilated if it loses touch with its deepest beginnings. The mother and her psyche join in symbolic incest. This regressive tendency has positive value in that the ego dies and is reborn with new transforming qualities. Without this connection there is dissociation as the conscious attitude becomes alienated from the individual and collective contents of the uncon-scious. There is a **horizontal split** between conscious and unconscious processes. The ego is temporarily lost in the collective unconscious. The archetype of the Great Mother is sometimes good, nourishing and life giving, and sometimes bad, devouring and killing. The child who has not managed to personify the archetypal lives with the terror of these extremes. Jung suggests that extremely violent traumas probably bypass the conscious experience of the victim but affect the underlying 'psychoid' layers that are inaccessible to our limited psychic activity. The patient wants to get rid of the terrible feelings about himself so he becomes either dissociated from his feelings or dissociated from the memories of events within which those feelings originated. He is then isolated either from his own affect or from parts of the contents of his memory. Dissociation is about the collective unconscious, repression is not. It is a world, which has lost Winnicott's potential space - the place between fantasy and reality, between psyche and external reality, the place for creativity and the basis for all symbolic activity. This can be lost in two ways: - by a fall into the world of fantasy in which the ego is swallowed by the unconscious, or a fall into the world of reality where the ego loses touch with the self and with its archetypal substrate, causing a horizontal split between the layers of the psyche.

There can also be **vertical splitting**. Jung describes how complexes develop as fragments of the psyche and become "split off owing to traumatic influences or certain incompatible tendencies". An intensification of complexes could lead to "extensive multiple dissociation" in which complexes become "endowed with an indomitable life of their own" (Jung 1936:121). This is a vertical split that Jung experienced in his own personalities No1 and No 2 (Jung 1963:104).

The perverse person does not perceive the object of his desire as a total human being. Denial and splitting are defences that serve as a protection of the self but mean that reality has become distorted, parts having been separated off or lost to consciousness. Only certain parts of the other are addressed, although different and often opposite bits may be experienced at different times so that two possibilities are held in the mind but are beyond conscious recognition. Laplanche and Pontalis describe how a person can have two psychic attitudes towards external reality when faced with an instinctive demand. One takes into account the reality, the other denies it (Laplanche and Pontalis 1973:427). There can be splitting of the ego or the object through idealisation and denigration leading to part-object relating. Both idealisation and denigration are apparent in a number of categories of perverse acts e.g. exhibitionism, voyeurism, fetishism, transvestism, and paedophilia. The patient may have split affective impulses toward the mother, attempting to deal with the aggressive component through denial. Alternatively, the aggressive component can be projected onto the mother. The ego may displace the split off aggression into the self or the patient's own body. Often the patient's description of his mother indicates that she looked for narcissistic gratification from her child. This made her a neglectful and possibly abusive mother who depended on the child to satisfy her own needs rather than responding to the dependency needs of her child.

A further confusion for the child is the distortion of time and space. A normal understanding of himself in space is perverted by experience of inappropriate closeness or distance. This experience is mirrored by a corresponding lack of freedom in psychological or inner space. Grosz usefully describes the 'interiority' of the child's experience of time, which is gauged by the body and its inner workings (Grosz 1995:99). If this is so, the possibility of gradual development through time may become distorted by inadequacy or by intrusion. The child's development of subjectivity is interfered with, forcing an interior sense of linear time to become circular time. In his inner world the child is constantly returning to the same place.

CHAPTER TWO

Deception

Perversion involves a, predominantly unconscious, refusal to give up deception. An appreciation of deception could be seen as the foundation stone of psychodynamic understanding since it plays such an important part in the life of the unconscious mind both in wakefulness and in dreaming. It is also the central theme in the myth of Oedipus. This myth has a depth of meaning for us many centuries after it was first recorded because it is timeless. Humanity embraces deception, so the myth speaks to our own nature. Steiner put forward a good case for not interpreting Sophocles' play in terms of the bravery of a victim of fate who gradually learns the unacceptable truth about himself (such as a patient might do in psychotherapy). Instead he emphasised another sort of conscious/unconscious split. The chief characters in the play must all have 'known' the identity of Oedipus, but had their own reasons for 'not realising' what was going on and not appreciating that Oedipus had committed parricide and incest. The other characters knew about Oedipus but seemed not to know they knew. Their experience and knowledge were at odds and had come together to deceive rather than to inform (Steiner 1985).

As in the myth, deception is about knowing and not knowing and of trying to make sense of different combinations of knowledge and experience. Ogden refers to the Oedipus myth saying, "Not knowing deprives us of our sense of who we are, and yet to know is to see that which we cannot bear to see" (Ogden 1989:3). This is the human condition.

For any species with predators, deceit is an essential skill for well being and even for survival. For lower species the deceit tends to be manifest on the outside, involving a change of appearance. A change of colour can determine life or death, an apparent enlargement of body size by bristling fur can frighten off an attacker. Human beings do the same sorts of things in a more complex way. From the age of about three or four years when we begin to develop a theory of mind, we begin to learn that a certain amount of lying and deception is part of a mature negotiation with the world.

> "Lying and self-deception permeate all aspects of human life and social interactions. Societal messages about deceit are often contradictory; we teach our children how to lie effectively and encourage others to lie to us even as we condemn lying as a vice" (Ford, 1995, p. 21)

Very good, or one might say very bad, deception has elaborate twists and double twists and often a sense of spatial displacement. The following is an example from work with a patient who was brought up by sexually abusive parents but managed, at some cost, to keep her sexually perverse internalised figures within her inner world rather than allowing them to act out.

Ms S

Ms S described her dislike of the wallpaper she had chosen for a room in her house because it was "imitation" stencilling and therefore was not only bad taste but would be "seen through" by other people. I suggested that the badness she felt was about her own ability to deceive. She then admitted that she had chosen the wallpaper because it looked like the "real" stencilling in blue and yellow on my wallpaper. She felt she had stolen it from me. In fact, the stencilling in my house was not on the wallpaper and was not blue and yellow but a single, different, colour. She had transposed it, and then polarised the one colour into two on opposing sides of the colour circle. I suggested that she might be telling me about some other deception, somewhere else. In the next session she "confessed" (her word) that she had started having private tuition in the hope of escaping abroad from her current occupation (and from me). She therefore felt she was stealing from me in spending her money in this way rather then offering to pay me a higher fee. She could not believe that I would allow her to have anything for herself. In other words, I would steal from her if she did not steal from me first. We were polarised, like the blue and yellow, into the depriver and the deprived. Her needs would only be met by being the one who deprived and deceived me.

Sometimes we can feel unsure as to whether those in authority are protecting us or are out to get us. A television documentary aptly called " Someone to Watch Over Me" (Yorkshire Television, 1999) investigated the child-minding function of Covert Video Surveillance (CVS) in the children's wards of hospitals. The systems were set up to monitor parents who might harm their children but ethical issues arise about deceiving anxious parents about the systems and filming them without their consent.

Perhaps we live in a world in which everyone knows they are being deceived but they are not necessarily sure who are the deceivers and who is trustworthy and honest, or even if total honesty is such a good thing. In March 2000 when Ken Livingstone went back on his promise not to stand for election as Mayor of London against an official Labour candidate, the news was headlined in a national newspaper as 'Trust me, I admit I'm a Liar'. In a democracy we choose who is in charge, so can we trust the government? In 1996 creationists in the Tennessee legislature argued for a law to ban the teaching of evolution as fact. The bill was narrowly voted down. At the same time New Hampshire considered whether evolutionary theory should be taught without parental consent. This fundamentalist attitude towards the integration of science with religious belief is a double deception. It denies the ability of the psyche to symbolise and it also suggests that God the creator deliberately laid down deceptive scientific evidence to suggest mankind came about through evolutionary development.

But how true is the truth? The novelist Beryl Bainbridge said (of her novel contending for the Booker prize), "Truth is a lie that has never been found out". So perhaps truth is just an assumption in the here and now that may change over time. Throughout history science has developed in paradigms, i.e. mutually exclusive frames of reference, theories and methods of ordering, examining and explaining the world. The ruling paradigm determines not only the concepts, theories and methods acceptable but what counts as a problem. These frames are dictators to be overthrown and replaced.

The Parts and the Whole

We use theory to explain, e.g. why a stick 'looks as if' it bends in water. The theory of optics tells as why. Traditionally science has been counter-intuitive, it denies unconscious processes. The idea that humans are rational beings and that their ideas, motivations and principal concerns are reasoned and reasonable has long been disputed. Jung was one in a long line of advocates for a more balanced understanding of the psyche in which thinking has its place, along with intuition, feeling and sensation as modes of processing and understanding information from outer and inner worlds.

We could think of the human mind working as a more or less integrated rational system with blips here and there that need to be ironed out for the efficient functioning of the whole. Rorty has suggested that a more accurate model of the mind would be **a set of relatively independent, loosely integrated subsystems** (Rorty 1988:12). This model allows for deception of parts of the self by other parts, the degree of self-deception representing the lack of integration of parts into the whole. Redfearn uses a similar model in describing parts of the self as **sub-personalities** that relate to each other, argue and co-operate like characters in a play which corresponds with the total person. The ability of the feeling of 'I' to move flexibly between sub-personalities can characterise psychological health, but when two internal characters become perversely locked the psyche is in danger and may turn destructively on others (Redfearn 1985:88). This appeared to have happened with the serial killer Dennis Nilsen who lured young men to his home and performed bizarre rituals on their bodies, which he later dismembered. He blamed his killings on a loveless childhood. It seemed that his 'dead self' was projected onto his victims whom he then looked after. He was aware of being both the carer and the person being cared for in his fantasy. The fixation of his fantasies powerfully transformed violence and mutilation into warmth and care.

Self-deception can certainly be a corrupting influence on the psyche, demanding further deception to cover up the cover-up and leading to more and more rigidity and denial throughout the system. Johnson calls self-deception "motivated belief in the face of contrary evidence" (Johnson 1988: 67). Psychoanalysis was built upon an understanding of self-deception. Freud's picture of the unconscious was a repository of repressed wishes and desires, in other words, a tool for self-deception. For Jung the unconscious was not such a dirty place. With its huge depths in a collective past, he respected it as the source and hope of the future, a place of creativity as well as darkness and despair. I think it would be wrong to think that psychotherapy and analysis are about freeing ourselves from deception, even self-deception. The idea that we can truly know ourselves might itself be a deception. What we work at in psychotherapy is balancing our self-knowledge with our deception, allowing ourselves to be a little bit blind here and there and a little bit dishonest, accepting that our shadows are valuable and should never be burnt out by the dazzling sun of idealism. The danger comes when we loose the flexibility to play with our shadows. Either we deny that we have a shadow, and so lessen ourselves, or we fall into our shadow and lose ourselves. Part of psychological growth has to be the acknowledgement that illumination creates shadows.

Deception has its uses. As an animal needs camouflage to protect its body from harm, humans need both conscious defences, such as lying, and unconscious defences, to protect our vulnerable psyches. We try to achieve a balance between deceiving others, like Hamlet's uncle Claudius, who could "Smile and smile and be a villain", and deceiving ourselves, which Dostoevsky described as more deeply ingrained in our nature than the deceit of others. Self-deception immediately falls foul of any idea of us as rational beings, but it does fit with a psychological model comprising less integrated subsystems, which lack full knowledge of each other. In perversion, I would suggest that the armoury amassed to protect vulnerable subsystems of the psyche is formidable. Equally formidable is the task of living in a paradoxical state of self-deception, in which the deceiver is in an unconscious collusive relationship with the deceived part of himself, thus allowing the deception to continue. Seductively paraphrased, "There are some frauds so well conducted that it would be stupidity not to be deceived by them" (Colton, 1825).

The dramatist, Tom Stoppard, allowed us to enter into the experience of our many competing and contradictory selves in his play 'The Real Inspector Hound' (Stoppard 1968). In this detective drama, it is unclear throughout the play whether any one of the characters is really the person they are supposed to be or whether they are 'in role' in their relationship with the other characters. Is the police inspector actually the dead body, is the stranger actually the lord of the house; does "I'll kill you if you ..." reflect a teasing friendship or deadly enmity? This even applies to the audience who might themselves be the players or be looking at a reflection of themselves. Because of the fluidity and changing perspective of the predominating theme of deception, it is difficult to decide what you are looking at because you are not able to say, "From where I am standing it looks like ...". The playwright ensures that your standpoint and frame of reference are as untrustworthy as your outlook. Therefore, any one part of the play has a shifty, unreal flavour that symbolises in microcosm the quality of the play as a whole.

As with all deceptions, we have to decide what is a part and what is the whole that it represents. How do we make correct inferences about other people and the world about us from our piecemeal experiences? I think that we do this through our understanding of patterns in our bodies and our psyches. We might have names for these patterns such as rhythms, repetitions, fixations, complexes or archetypes. The patterning is not neutral; it is dynamic, wanting to express itself as part of our being, or personality and our bodily functioning, and it is most resistant to attempts to overrule it (Ross 1998:241).

Attacks on Linking

Psychotherapy is structured as a series of encounters between therapist and patient that facilitate the building of a relationship of evolving complexity. During each session the psychotherapist makes inferences about the psychic structure of the patient from the experience of engagement with him. Judgements have to be made about the extent to which each experience of the patient is, as it were, a unique chip off the block of the patient's personality, and the extent to which it is more like a fractal, a picture of the whole patient in microcosm. When our judgement and intuition lead us to understand that we have experienced a symbolic expression of the whole, or an important larger aspect of the patient, we are likely to feel able to make an interpretation. We would share this with the patient if the time were felt to be right, i.e. if the patient had sufficient understanding of his own pattern to accept and incorporate a transcendent link between the part and the whole. The perverse patient is likely to be **extremely resistant to accepting such links**. His unconscious need is to keep the whole fragmented and experienced only through its constituent parts and on separated levels.

The espousal of deception allows, and even fuels, the continuation of this fragmented psychic functioning. Deception offers a narrow and often dangerous path through life but is sometimes unconsciously chosen as the best protection from anxiety. It provides a solution. It works, but it only works for a short time; therefore the patient's relationship to perversion becomes addictive. The gratifying solution is held deceptively in the mind and there is a great deal of investment in creating an elaborate golden path leading to this solution. The path itself becomes imbued with anticipatory excitement and assumes an important role both in fantasy and in the planning of perverse acts. As many advocates of blood sports protest, the sport is not about killing, it is about the chase. But it would be deceptive to deny that it is the hope of a kill that inspires the chase.

Deception and Defence

People may be inadvertently driven to perversion through their early experiences as victims. The deception of others, often parents or carers, who trick them out of their childhood, also makes them victims of their own deception. They may then enter into a sado-masochistic relationship with their own deceptiveness. This might condemn them to a world of self-deception in which the perverse solution is upheld as life-giving. The psychic health of others is then also at risk if the patient sadistically inflicts his perverse sexuality onto others. If this happens the balance has been lost. Deception is no longer a tool for integration, to help the patient on the path to individuation. It now opposes psychological growth, encouraging him to cut off, separate and deny. Through lack of balance the patient loses a sense of centre and of self. The patterns of the psyche and the body are in increasing tension. Instead of a mandala with radiating complementary patterning, the parts of the pattern have lost a sense of contributing to the whole but are vying to shine as separate fragments in the limelight.

Escher

The graphic artist M. C. Escher (1898-1972) had a remarkable sense of how to represent and communicate the psychological assurance and inner feeling of stability gained by the experience of symmetry. He demonstrated the efforts to which the psyche will go if its sense of symmetry is challenged. He recorded 17 types of symmetry in 2 dimensions and 230 types in 3 dimensions. He had an appreciation of the deceptive nature of realism in art knowing that, paradoxically, the realistic appearance of a picture is achieved by deceiving the viewer. For example, artistic convention demands that three-dimensional objects retain their appearance of solid form even when presented on a two dimensional surface. In fact, many people judge the quality of art by how well they are deceived. Escher spent much of his life working on this paradoxical relationship between art and the reality we believe to exist in the outside world. One way in which he did this was to explore the relationship between part and whole images. He developed three tessellated images: equilateral triangles, squares and hexagons. These are the three tessellations of Euclidian geometry, the geometry of the three dimensional space in which we live. These tessellated forms, usually of humans and animals could expand indefinitely across the Euclidean plane, forming an infinite pattern rather than an object. To create a whole object, he found that he needed to make the tessellar elements smaller as he worked outwards in each successive round. These were regular tessellations of the non-Euclidean plane, a branch of mathematics that investigates the geometry of theoretical spaces with four or more dimensions, known as the hyperbolic plane. Escher was not a mathematician, but he used his artistic talent and his incredible preoccupation with the relationship between unconscious understanding of form and its effect on visual perception to widen his perspective. It was through intuition that he arrived at a convention used in non-Euclidean geometry, the Poincare Disc. The tessellar elements in the disc appear larger in the centre and become smaller and curved towards the outer limits of the disc, until they reach a limit forming a whole object image.

In our work as analysts and psychotherapists with perverse patients, we are often looking at the edge of the Poincare Disc. This is the area in which the tessellated images, which might have been familiar to us in a simpler form, become distorted and less recognisable. It is not so easy for us to relate to the structures of theory and experience that we have established. This means that we can easily be deceived by what we come across in our patients. Rather than seeing it as a distorted part of the whole, we may try to flatten the part to make it more familiar and give it a better fit. Instead we need to try to find the bends and distortions at the edges of our own understanding, so that we stretch, twist and turn our own comprehension to develop an understanding of what we experience.

Criminality

Deception is pervasive. It is not unusual for a patient who comes for psychotherapy because of concerns about sexual acting out, also to be involved in deceptive or criminal activities that appear to be of an entirely different kind. In most criminal activities the symptoms are not necessarily overtly

erotic although they may reflect the workings of a perverse
personality structure. The gains of criminality are then
likely to be more for the satisfaction of the unconscious than
the conscious mind. Some burglaries are of this kind, where
the intrusion, destruction and spoiling are more important
that the theft. Glasser relates the case of a burglar who:

> "would impulsively run amok in the house he
> was in the process of burgling: he would pull
> out all the contents of cupboards and drawers,
> rip clothing to pieces, slash cushions, hurl pieces
> of furniture about the room, and run through
> the rooms throwing flour, sugar, eggs and such
> things wherever he went. Finally he would leave
> the house without taking any of its valuables.
> The analysis of his housebreaking revealed that
> the main motives involved were those of the core
> complex. He would burgle at times when he felt
> particularly lonely. Entering the house represented
> entering his mother's body, and taking its valuables
> represented forcibly acquiring her precious love of
> which she had been so ungiving in his childhood"
> (Glasser, 1979, p. 289).

Legally anyone who commits a crime is considered to be
acting with conscious intent and therefore to be responsible
for his actions. This puts our understanding of the psyche
into a paradoxical position in relation to the law. A criminal
is not considered to be acting with unconscious intent or
to be the victim of a horizontal split between his conscious
and unconscious mind unless he is diagnosed as insane at
the time of the crime. The most obvious type of deceptive
crime is by white-collar workers and the perpetrators are
generally not apprehended. Examples are embezzlement,
insurance and real estate frauds. This sort of criminal is
often charming, engaging and convincing; qualities which
can stand them in good stead if they ever reach a court of

law. They are protected by not necessarily conforming to any common stereotype of a criminal. With this type of crime it may be difficult meaningfully to associate the criminal with the crime (why would *he* do a thing like that) without considering the unconscious narcissistic gratification that may be gained by getting one over on someone else.

Sometimes a minor deception proves to be the tip of a deceptive iceberg. In 1999 the police and academic staff from the University of Huddersfield made the discovery that one of the best places to track down criminals was a disabled parking bay. A joint police/academic sting in the centre of the town recorded the registration numbers of all cars parking in disabled bays without orange stickers. The numbers were checked through the police national computer. One third of illegal parkers were found to have criminal records, half had committed previous road traffic offences, and a fifth were of immediate interest to the police investigating unsolved crimes. One fifth of the cars had been used previously in, or linked with, thefts, drugs or other offences.

A terrifying example of the perverse psychic structure in action is seen in the life and crimes of Fred West, who sexually abused, murdered and mutilated his children and others whom he lured to his home. He tended to treat people as objects, often as sexual objects. When questioned by the police he did not know his children's names and could not distinguish between them. He could remember almost none of the names of the people he had murdered. They were carcasses to be disposed of once their usefulness to him had finished. He called the bodies of murdered people 'it' whereas he often called objects 'he'. He had an obsession with holes and passages and wanted to see inside woman's bodies. He was obsessed with size and with putting big things into small holes. (He unnecessarily cut up bodies to fit them into small holes).

"What was striking about Fred West's account of how he had murdered and mutilated his daughter was the way in which the close details of how exactly he had decapitated and dismembered Heather and disposed of her remains frequently slipped into animated soliloquies on ordinary household things. With a sort of compulsion, a description of cutting or carrying would turn, within one or two sentences, into a listing or inventory of the objects he had done the cutting or carrying – or tying or washing or concealing – with." (Burn, 1998, p. 336)

Fred West's childhood was sexually abusive and chaotic. It was rumoured that he lost his virginity to his mother at the age of 12 and was possibly abused by his father. At 19 he was charged with having sex with his 13-year-old sister and being the father of her baby. She refused to give evidence against him and the case was dropped. His mother spoke in his defence.

CHAPTER THREE

The Trickster

"All Cretans are liars"
(attributed to a semi-legendary poet and priest
who may have lived in Crete around the seventh
century BC)

How do we understand the truth of this statement made
by a Cretan? In trying to comprehend, we are led back
and forth and then outside to another order of reality that
throws us once again into an infinite cycle of self-contradic-
tion. This self-referential paradox, with its frustrating sense
of illusionary truth, is what we are up against in trying to
understand perversion. There are many part-truths and
many inferences that seem to lead to the whole truth, but
the parts contradict the whole and any one part seems to
contradict another. Focussing on any one type of countertransference feeling or particular characteristic of the patient
as a key to understanding, can lead to a feeling that the rest
does not fit, so we shift focus again and another part of the
whole is thrown into the area of disbelief. This scenario of
conflict, of reversal, of confusion and riddles, of deceit and
passion is the amoral, mythological playground of the gods,
where games are played out with omnipotence, impulsive-

ness and intensity. It is the killing field for the archetype of
the Trickster, the deadly clown. The rewards are slippery
and ephemeral. The Trickster dupes others and is always
duped himself. Who is this Trickster and what is he, or she,
up to?

> "The Trickster is at one and the same time creator
> and destroyer, giver and negator . . . He wills
> nothing consciously. At all times he is constrained
> to behave as he does from impulses over which he
> has no control. He knows neither good nor evil yet
> he is responsible for both. He possesses no values,
> moral or social, is at the mercy of his passions and
> appetites, yet through him creations and values
> come into being" (Radin, 1973, p. xxiii)

Jung described the Trickster as "both subhuman and
superhuman, a bestial and divine being, whose chief and
most alarming characteristic is his unconsciousness" (Jung
1954:263). And again:

> "The so-called civilised man has forgotten the
> Trickster. He remembers him only figuratively
> and metaphorically, when, irritated by his own
> ineptitude, he speaks of fate playing tricks on him
> or of things being bewitched. He never suspects
> that his own hidden and apparently harmless
> shadow has qualities whose dangerousness
> exceeds his wildest dreams" (Jung, 1954, p.267)

The Trickster does not hold the opposites in tension,
but falls into them. The appearance of pure good hides the
greatest threat of falling into evil. One of the most familiar
examples of such falling into the opposite is seen in the spell
of the contrasexual archetype. The playwright Dennis Potter
is particularly skilled in the portrayal of the seductive anima
figure whose unconscious lure leaves men powerless and

at her mercy. Those who have read or seen Potter's play "Karaoke" (Potter, 1996), will recall the clever, imaginative, lateral thinking author, Daniel Field, who is plagued by the sickness of his body (as was the author himself). Field falls for his opposite, the beautiful, brainless, literal thinking Sandra Sollars, (played in the television version by the same actress as another anima figure in Potter's earlier television production, "Lipstick on your Collar" (Potter, 1993)). Both plot and relationships are presented amidst an inner-outer world confusion so that even the reader or viewer loses a sense of personal identity and can only submit to the determinism of the archetype, or the Karaoke soundtrack.

Moving to the consulting room, I would like to refer to a particular case in which just such opposites came into play.

Mr A

Mr A's profession involved him in the treatment of bodily ailments. When taking part in emergency helicopter rescues, he experienced feelings of sadistic excitement, particularly about those who were most vulnerable. Although he did not act on these feelings immediately, they perturbed him, and after such a rescue he would feel the need to cross-dress: to dress up in what he described as "tarty women's clothes" and masturbate to reach sexual satisfaction. This patient could retrieve only sketchy memories from his early life but he did remember cross-dressing in this manner as far back as early childhood. One vivid incident that he recalled was of soiling his pants and being laughed at by his parents and by visitors. A classic interpretation might be that this patient's cross-dressing was a hostile mimicry of womanhood, directed in retaliatory attack towards his humiliating mother. However, teasing out the details of this patient's own fantasies, the most prominent association was his need to attract his father. He fantasised that he was dressing up as the sort of women his father 'really' fancied and would prefer to his mother. He saw himself as identifying with his father's anima. John Beebe describes how a father's unacknowledged anima can be imposed upon his son. In the biblical story, Jacob, himself a trickster, idealised his son Joseph, who reminded him of the wife he had lost. Jacob's passion throws his son into the familiar story of tricksterish adventure, sexual encounter, danger and intrigue (Beebe 1984:277).

Mr A felt unable to work out his conflicts in the outer world in which he was small and vulnerable, so retreated to the safety of his inner world. Then, like the Trickster, he could change clothes and shapes and experience deceptive omnipotence. This patient also demonstrated his tricksterish capacity within the analytic sessions. He would sometimes attribute a feeling or opinion of mine to "us", meaning him and me, or state what "we" might be about to do. My immediate inner response was to draw back, experiencing a loss or even theft, as if he was taking me over and tricking me out of part of my individuality. My interpretation to him was that his difficulty in dealing with me encouraged him to clothe himself in my feelings or opinions in order to experience us as together, and to avoid conflict between us (although unconsciously he incited it).

This leads to another important point Radin makes about the Trickster: that figures connected to him, the people, the animals, the various supernatural beings and monsters, can all adopt the qualities of the Trickster, and perversely assume alternative identities and values. If this is so, what happens when the analyst is thrown into the amoral, unstable world of the Trickster? If perversion is a temptation in the mind common to us all, perhaps the analyst is tempted towards professional perversion. This will be explored in Chapter 6 but it might be helpful to recognise the Trickster in the history of our own profession. After the split between Freud and Jung, Freud felt that his 'son and heir' had betrayed him and that Jung had been swept off with 'the black tide of occultism'. Jung experienced the same sort of tricksterish betrayal by Freud. As Casement writes:

> "It is not difficult to discern whom Jung is really alluding to when he writes of Yahweh: 'With his touchiness and suspiciousness the mere possibility of doubt was enough to infuriate him and induce the peculiar double-faced behaviour of which he had already given proof in the Garden of Eden, when he pointed out the tree to the First Parents and at the same time forbade them to eat of it'."
> (Casement, 1998, p. 74)

Both Freud and Jung might be accused of being Trickster fathers to their followers. Freud apparently worked to bring to conscious examination, and give an honest and open account of, denied and repressed sexual desires and motivations. But he left many would-be adherents in the 'All Cretans are liars' position in that the strength of Freud's belief in the truth of his theories of sexuality reflected on his own motivations for developing a sexual basis for his psychology. Paradoxically, Freud's detailed exposure of sexuality might have been a reflection of his own sexual prudery.

Jung saw the Trickster as god, man and animal in one. He compared the Trickster with the alchemical figure of Mecurius, half beast, half-divine. With his malicious pranks and shape shifting he was both sub and super-human (Jung 1954:255). Trickster qualities are found in the two Norse gods Odin and Loki. Odin is given to *interfering with* people, (a term used to describe some forms of sexually perverse acting out). He attracts and charms people, but has no interest in their welfare, so treats them as puppets for his own desires. He is known for his treachery, betraying the trust that he encourages others to place in him. Loki is a more developed Trickster who amuses and beguiles. He is motivated by impulse and gets himself in half-comical adventures and complications. The types of trustful/ mistrustful relationships formed by both gods are familiar to the consulting room.

The Trickster figure is common to the mythology of many ancient cultures including Greece, China and Japan. Paul Radin describes how many of the trickster's traits are perpetuated in the figures of the medieval jester, Punch and Judy and the clown. The Trickster in American Indian mythology is the creator/destroyer who wills nothing consciously but acts on his own uncontrollable impulses. He is amoral in that he possesses no moral or social values and is at the mercy of his passions and appetites. He is an inchoate with no fixed shape or form, so those around him find him difficult to recognise or contain. Significantly for the psychotherapist, Radin states that the Trickster figure becomes intelligible and meaningful if we view it as an attempt at personal problem solving, both inner and outer. Here is the positive side of this slippery elusive presence in the consulting room. If we can experience the trickster at work as a communication from patient to analyst (and sometimes the other way round), we find that every deceit is also a truth and every diversion becomes a hopeful lead. Jung described all mythical figures as corresponding to inner psychic experiences and originally springing from them. Understandably, this makes the Trickster patient fascinating to the psychotherapist who is invited into an unboundaried, amoral playground.

Narcissism and Excitement without Reflection

One aspect of the Trickster archetype which links it with perversion is that the Trickster's clever dissembling never offers more than a temporary solution. The tricks and deceptions have to be repeated and reinvented every time the instinct or impulse demands satisfaction. Significantly the Trickster is very much in his body and uses his body in his trickery. Body parts are often dissociated. The creativity of the Trickster lies in the endless solutions he concocts to meet his own narcissistic needs. Like the perverse personality, he constantly delights in his plans and plots. If he stopped to reflect on himself he might experience the opposite of this – the loss of real relationship. This was the fate of Narcissus who was told by the seer that he would live to a ripe old age only if he never knew himself. The arrogance with which he spurned the advances of others, including the nymph Echo, led to his gradual demise. The punishment of the goddess Nemesis was that he should experience unrequited love. In other words, he would spend the rest of his life reflecting on the image of himself in the water until he eventually died of grief. The conception of Narcissus was through non-consensual sex, (his mother Liriope was imprisoned and ravished by the river-god Cephisus). He was tricked into life and tricked out of it and during his life he tricked others by the beauty of his outward appearance. He had no ability to enter into reciprocal relationships.

The Scandinavian folk tale of Princess Cottongrass has a similar theme. The young princess leaves her parents, the King and Queen, and asks Leap the elk to 'carry her into life'. She is tricked by the elves and the witch of the woods into losing her crown and her dress. The elk is also tricked by her presentation of young innocence and carries her naked on his back. Finally the loss she has denied is concretised when the chain with a golden heart, which her mother gave her on the day she was born, drops from her neck into the water and disappears. Like Narcissus, she stares into the water looking for her lost heart until she is turned into a flower.

Aspects of the narcissistic character are found in different personalities. They can be dominant, or part of a psychological pattern. It might be useful to think of narcissistic disturbance not as a diagnostic category but rather as a dimension of the human psyche in general. Narcissistic disturbance can arise when the infant cannot believe he gives 'the other', generally the mother, a good experience. His reaction may be to withdraw, or to force himself on the other – both involve a lack of mutuality. The major symptoms of pathological narcissism are lack of identity and of self-esteem and a turning to oneself as the erotic object. This was the fate of Narcissus. The stories of both Narcissus and Princess Cottongrass are about defective mirroring. Were they real-life characters, one might assume that neither had good early mirroring experiences that they were able to internalise. In such circumstances the ego has little capacity to mirror the self or the self to mirror the ego. Narcissus and Princess Cottongrass lived with a disconnected inner state but, tragically, when they were able to look at themselves in the mirroring water it was too late; they could only experience their loss. They had both sacrificed true relationship for a life of excitement and risk taking. It was the death-in-life of overwhelming sorrow and loss, in which infantile primary narcissism had been replaced by an idealisation of their own pre-genital state. In Freudian terms this was their Ego Ideal. They both utilised the defence of splitting through idealisation and devaluation. (The beautiful flower of the Narcissus also stinks). They were cut off horizontally from their unconscious but their ego was also split vertically. Princess Cottongrass lost bits of her identity, her crown, her dress, her golden heart, she ran away with the animal part of herself, but then, because of her lack of internalised parents she felt she had nothing, she had lost her heart. Finally her grief caused her to lose her humanity and her human life. It is a story of both loneliness and omnipotence. It parallels the tale of Narcissus whose ego inflation, investment in his own beauty, strength and allure caused him to ignore his weaknesses – he only experienced his own vulnerability in 'the timid deer' which he then had to hunt down and kill. Here there was a horizontal split between the conscious attitude and that of the unconscious.

This is reminiscent of the story of two teenage gangs rivalling for supremacy. They engaged in a fight that resulted in a number of minor injuries. It had nearly broken up when one youth was knocked to the ground. As he lay defenceless, a member of the other gang lunged in and stabbed him to death. Why did he do this? He later explained that he could not bear the other young man's weakness and vulnerability. When faced with his own shameful qualities, which he projected onto his helpless victim, he had to attack and destroy in the other what he could not stand in himself. The same dynamic was evident in the notorious killing a few years ago of the toddler James Bulger who was taken from a shopping centre by two young boys while his mother's attention was distracted. His abductors probably did not intend to kill him but said that they could not stand his crying. "Why wouldn't he stop?" "Why wouldn't he just lie down?" So they threw stones at him. He did not stop crying so they threw more stones. . . . . I suspect the two attackers had shed tears enough themselves. Like Narcissus they only wanted the best of themselves to be mirrored back.

Was Narcissus a pervert? Perhaps this is a perverse question since it falsely brings together what is separate – the mythical character from the collective unconscious, Narcissus, with the concept of 'pervert' which comes from the structure of society's moral, ethical and legal framework. The question does what perversion always does, it crosses uncrossable boundaries in an attempt to create a world of sameness, where boundaries of age, sex, part/whole, willing/unwilling are the same. There is an abolition of difference, particularly of opposites. It is a world of fantasy in which one person's fantasies are imposed on an unwilling other. Perversion implies an inability to obtain genital satisfaction. It involves a deep split between genital and pre-genital sexuality. The person feels increasing tension that can only be relieved by pre-genital perverse action. Paedophilic behaviour is pre-genital; it characterises a person who has not reached full sexual maturity. This contrasts with incest, in which the perpetrator has usually attained genital maturity but regresses in the incestuous act.

Similarly, it would make nonsense of the tale of Princess Cottongrass to accuse her of indecent exposure, because princesses are archetypal figures who can do all sorts of things in fairy tales that the rest of us are not permitted to do in the real world. Her reckless journey on the elk leaves her with feelings of shame. She is not so much guilty about her actions as ashamed of her whole self and her loss of faith in her ego-ideal. This is the sort of shame experienced by patients with perverse qualities. The person who reverts to exhibitionistic behaviour has low self-esteem and tends to be depressed. He or she does not become overtly angry or destructive but draws attention to himself. The excitement of the other temporarily relieves the depression. There is a difficulty in forming positive reciprocal relationships with others with a tendency to be either over-compliant or over-challenging. In Freudian terms, there is a sado-masochistic relationship with the super-ego. The apprehension and punishment that may ensue can also be experienced as rewarding, giving a masochistic satisfaction.

Neville Symington usefully describes this destructive attempt to meet ones narcissistic needs as turning away from the lifegiver (Symington 1993:41). Jung stressed how narcissistic problems could be seen as positive, as symptoms of a new self-image. But with the perverse solution the narcissist turns away from the lifegiver and is no longer motivated by hope but by an unconscious suicidal intent - nearly always the result of early trauma, possibly cumulative trauma causing the person to push away the infant self. A damaged early attachment system combines with dissociated memories of traumatic experiences leading to simmering narcissistic rage. When there is a trigger this leads to violence and re-enactment.

Attachment

Perversion could be seen as attachment that has not developed, but has twisted and set. The bond of attachment no longer supports progress and development so the person lives in a world that has lost Winnicott's potential space; the place between fantasy and reality, between psyche and external reality, the place for creativity and the basis for all symbolic activity. The rich creative fantasy world of the unconscious can no longer support the ego in the real world and the ego is left to act blindly, unable to feed its unconscious substrate.

In the relationship between the psychotherapist and the patient it would probably be wrong to suppose that the truth of a person's biography gradually unfolds, if by truth we mean that which an observer might record as objective fact. What actually comes to the fore is a piecemeal of seemingly significant images and narratives, which are aroused within the relationship and have their own attachments and rational and irrational colourings from every level of consciousness. It is not the job of the psychotherapist to don the hat of a forensic scientist and look for evidence to verify the patient's creative productions. What is needed is the identification and shared recognition of patterns and themes within the patient's life story as it opens up in the transference relationship so that these can be knitted into an understanding of the patient's inner world.

The Body

The patterns and themes of the perverse psyche are enacted through the body. Johnson calls this body-mind connection 'The Body in the Mind'. He explores the part played by the body in the establishment of meaning:

> "The body has been ignored because reason has been thought to be abstract and transcendent, that is, not tied to any of the bodily aspects of human understanding. The body has been ignored because it seems to have no role in our reasoning about abstract subject matters." (Johnson, 1987, p. xiv)

He refers to the *embodiment* of human understanding:

> "The view I am proposing is this: in order for us to

have meaningful, connected experiences that we can comprehend and reason about, there must be pattern and order to our actions, perceptions, and conceptions. A schema is a recurrent pattern, shape and regularity in, or of, these ongoing ordering activities. These patterns emerge as meaningful structures for us chiefly at the level of our bodily movements through space, our manipulation of objects, and our perceptual interactions." (Johnson, 1987, p. 29)

Mr E

Mr E dressed almost exclusively in second-hand clothes. He was not uninterested in his appearance or unable to buy new clothes, in fact the opposite was true. He took great delight and much time and effort trawling second-hand shops for attractive bargains. Very frequently his first comment in a session would be about his appearance, the choice of clothes that day and how the combination of garments had been selected to give the right look. Now this man was brought up living in humble circumstances by a mother who invested her ambitions in her son. He was clever, which brought him privileges in education and later in his career, but it was important for his mother that his clothes were also perfect and that he was a cut above the neighbouring children. Although pleasant-looking as an adult, when a boy he did not like his appearance. I think he experienced a deception in being the boy whose body was made to look smart, but who saw himself as falsely presented. There was a distorted mirroring between his inner and outer selves. As an adult he continued the trickery in his appearance but for his own ends. He bought his clothes cheaply but very carefully and thoughtfully. He opted out of the conventional fashion scene, at the same time challenging and devaluing. He created for himself something that no one else could easily follow but that he could admire in himself, which brought interested and admiring comments and which enabled him to look down on the suckers who fell for commercialism. He felt he had won. But this patient never won for more than a short time. He found how the trick could take over the trickster.

The process of human development, maturation and education offer the potential for an almost indefinite elaboration and colouring of inner patterns or schemata. This will continue to happen in a positive way provided that the process is nurtured and stimulated appropriately. If it is neglected, overburdened or assaulted by trauma which cannot be fully understood or incorporated into the immature schema, the course of development will be perverted and further maturation will be patchy and distorted with parts of the schema frozen in an undeveloped state. If this happens in the course of an individual's sexual development, full genital maturity will not be achieved, and at least parts of the psyche will become fixated at a pregenital level. The emerging adult is then sexually mature in the physical sense but in his psyche he is still prepubescent and he is likely to experience sexual fulfilment through child-adult contact either in fantasy or in the outer world. In any couple, his part could be either that of the 'child' or of the other, the person who is sexually excited only by the vulnerability and immature sexuality of the child partner through a projection of his own inner state. This may become a rigid and dynamic pattern that absorbs the psyche in planning and seeking fulfilment.

The final chapter will look at the role of the psychotherapist in helping the patient to harness the archetypal energy of the Trickster and turn it from a path of destruction.

CHAPTER FOUR

Female Perversion

Psychotherapists learn to respond to the whole patient using the language of the body as well as the mind. As the antics of the Trickster demonstrate, perverse structures and strategies involve both body and mind. *Sexual* perversion in particular is the embodiment of psychic conflict. The body acts to resolve the conflict and diminish anxiety through sexual action. The relationship between the psyche (all the psychic processes) and the body is complex and often mysterious. The history of philosophy is full of attempts to find a suitable mind-body model. We have come a long way since Plato, and later Descartes, postulated the separateness of body and mind. Continuity of the body-mind system with dynamic interactive flow within it is supported by research in the natural sciences. Pert suggests that mind itself is the information flowing among bodily parts and that it is mind that holds the network together (Pert 1987:3). The Nobel laureate Roger Sperry described consciousness as an emergent property of the whole system that could not be predicted by its parts. He considered that the central control power of the belief system of an individual had potential control over social behaviour and possible health consequences (Sperry 1986:423). He implied that the experi-

47

ence of purpose and meaning exerted a downward control over the properties at a physiological and physical level. This certainly seems to be so in perversion, when desire dictates belief.

One obvious problem in establishing a body-mind or body-psyche model is that male and female systems must necessarily vary. Any network or system reflecting or integrating the system of the physical body must allow for differences in gender. Robert Stein (1973) describes the rational mind as having a place but says we need to allow it to be instructed by nature, not the other way round. We cannot speak of a specific somatic location, such as the brain, for the psyche or for the containing and guiding archetypes: they are in every cell of the body. The ego is not the directing energy and intelligence in the human person-ality, it is a mediator between archetype and external reality – the archetype is the directing principle. The ego informs, restrains and contains in order to give time for a reconcili-ation to be effected between inner and outer reality (Stein 1973:22).

The emphasis in previous chapters has been on the male, and most categorised sexual perversions are related to male sexuality and the male body. As the vast majority of known perpetrators of sexually perverse acts are men and likewise it is the men who, until very recently, have been the writers on this topic, it is no wonder that the male perspective has predominated. There is evidence, however, that a different mind-body model is needed to accommodate female sexual perversity.

Male and Female

Estela Welldon has contrasted the sexually perverse behaviour of men and women (Welldon 1988:19-41). The sexual organs of women are spread through the body, the whole female body is a sex organ, and therefore the whole body becomes the object of perversion. Like their sexual organs, women's private lives are more secret than those of men. Less is known about what women actually do and how they do it since they tend to be more contained inside their homes and inside their bodies. Perversion in males is viewed as the result of an unresolved Oedipus complex, which has castration anxiety as its central and main component. When the oedipal male reaches manhood, he is unable to reach genital primacy with a person of the opposite sex, since his mother is still in his unconscious mind and he fears castration by his father. In male perversion there is a split between what the individual experiences as his anatomical maturity, and his mental representations of his body in which he sees himself as a raging and desperate baby. His body is genital but his fantasies, centred on revenge, are pre-oedipal. By contrast, for the girl there is a feeling of not being safe with her mother whom she experiences as a dangerous person. She fears, through projection of her own envious feelings, that her mother will rob her of her reproductive capacities. Welldon quotes the work of Raphael-Leff (1983) who describes two basic models of mothering. First the 'regulator' in which the mother expects the baby to adapt to herself and secondly the 'facilitator' in which the mother adapts to the baby. She suggests that the facilitator mother with severe pathology who welcomes the infant's intense dependence and exclusive intimacy may bring up transvestite, fetishistic or transsexual boys. The pathological regulator mother might be the mother of battered babies. For Welldon, the main difference between male and female perverse action is in the aim. In men the act is aimed at an outside part-object, in woman it is usually against themselves, their bodies, or objects they see as their own creations – their babies. Bodies and babies are both treated as part-objects. Women's approach to sex is also different from that of men. Women seek sex for the whole of themselves; they want to be loved as people, whereas men want a sexual relationship in order to be sexually satisfied. Women's sexually perverse behaviour also tends to be more 'attached'. For example, flashing and other exhibitionistic behaviour tends to be directed towards close figures rather than strangers.

This inner-outer difference in the ways males and females express their perversity is probably also evident in other conditions. For example, girls with Asperger's Syndrome, a pervasive developmental disorder within the spectrum of autism, express themselves somewhat differently from boys. Their special interests may not be as conspicuous and intense as those of boys. Thus, they can be described as the 'invisible child' – socially isolated, preoccupied by their imaginary world but not a disruptive influence in the classroom. Their condition is often not diagnosed because they can easily be considered immature rather than odd. Boys, on the other hand, tend to act out with aggressive and disruptive behaviour and therefore are more likely to be referred to a specialist (McLennan, Lord and Schopler 1993).

Women and Criminality

The amount we know about women's sexually perverse behaviour is limited by the nature of womanhood and the limited extent to which woman clash with law enforcers in their sexual behaviour. Here again the inner/outer distinction applies. Women do not generally go out to commit crimes, including sexual crimes, as men do. They are also more likely to use their deceptive qualities to instigate criminal activity rather than be perpetrators themselves. At the time of writing there were 51,844 males in British prisons and only 3,078 women (H.M. Prison Service Statistics, April 2001). Even though these figures reflect a reluctance to send women to prison for indictable offences, it also indicates that women are not committing the types of crimes that send men to prison.

One woman now in prison is Rosemary West, who was married to Fred West, referred to in the last chapter. Rosemary was exhibitionistic, she liked being watched. She made Fred's 8-year-old son watch her both on the toilet and having sex. She also exposed her children by taking their pants down and smacking their bottoms when she was out shopping. Her relationship with Fred was complementary. He was a dominating voyeur. He videoed her having sex with other men but depersonalised her, keeping her head and face out of the picture, he was only interested in her sexual parts. She behaved like a slave in her masochistic submissions to him, which made her feel triumphant (Burn 1998:343).

Repetition

Perversion in women has the same addictive quality as in men. Anna Ornstein writes of her patient needing a sexual 'fix'. This was a patient who had an eroticised relationship with her father, which fell short of sexual intercourse but led her to feel that she, rather than her mother, was her father's chosen sexual partner:

> "The experiences with her father, in spite of their exploitative nature, were, in many ways, restorative; they had two important aspects to them: (1) the excitement of the interaction itself was enlivening, and (2) it was then that she felt most appreciated and valued. The tragedy was that the experiences that helped her overcome her apathy and listlessness were the very same ones, which created the symptomatic behaviour later in life. These prematurely sexually overstimulating and incestuous encounters became the prototypes by which she tried to overcome her depression and suicidal thoughts in adult life" (Ornstein, 1995, p. 111).

Mothering

Welldon (1988) describes the same sort of addictive behaviour in mothers' incestuous relationships with their infants and young children. The perverse mother uses her child as an object of her own perverse sexuality, becoming compulsively attached to the child as her exclusive sexual partner. This is normally a tragic reversal of the mother's exploitation by one of her own parents. The mother is perpetuating an incestuous cycle. Her child is not seen as a separate person but someone that gratifies her own needs.

A perverse relationship, without sexual content can develop if the mother needs the child to satisfy her own narcissistic needs. If the mother has grown up in at atmosphere of abuse or neglect, her low self esteem may cause her to seek 'mothering' from her own child. Such motivation can cause teenage girls who have little sense of a good internalised mother, perversely to seek motherhood themselves in order to experience themselves in a mothering relationship. This reversal of internal figures can lead to disastrous consequences for the next generation when the mother finds that her dolly/baby begins to have independent toddler needs and makes demands on the mother which she finds difficult to meet. It is hard for the mother to find that her child is not there for her but needs her to be there for him.

Furman (1992) conducted research in a therapeutic nursery established to help mothers to move from narcissistic investment in their children to object relationship. The rationale behind the project was that the child's mastering of his own body was the vehicle by which ownership of his body could be transferred from mother to child. The project was carefully structured into four stages of encouraging the mother to relinquish ownership of the child's body:

1) 'Doing' stage in which mother does for the child and the child enjoys it.
2) 'Doing with' stage in which the mother and child share tasks.
3) 'Standing by to admire' stage where the child does some things, or parts of tasks, for himself.
4) 'Doing for oneself' in which the child takes over mastery of the bodily task.

As the infants became more independent and competent in managing their own bodily needs they gradually came to be seen as separate people by their mothers. The children were also more secure as they had been given an internal sense of security rather than the lack of security provided by an over-protective mother. Holmes (1996) quotes a study using Ainsworth's strange situation test. In this test the attachment status of 1-year-olds is assessed by their response to a 3-minute separation from their caregiver. Ainsworth found that the parental responsiveness to infant affect was a key determinant of secure attachment. Fonagy (1991) found that the capacity to think about oneself in relation to others (reflexive self function or RSF) was a key determinant of whether mothers whose own childhoods were traumatic would have infants who turned out to be insecure in the strange situation. The capacity for RSF was a vital protection against psychological vulnerability.

Jane

My own patient, Jane, had been physically and sexually abused. She was her father's favourite and he selected her for sexual abuse from the age of about six years until puberty. He was usually drunk when he returned from the pub and climbed into her bed. These encounters were sometimes followed by gifts of small amounts of money that made Jane feel special. Her mother was an erratic and violent woman who simultaneously colluded with and resented her husband's interest in Jane. She would erupt in anger, often with no apparent cause and throw heavy objects or hot food at Jane. Sometimes she would beat her to the floor and kick her around the head. The kicking was so severe that it caused permanent brain damage and epileptic seizures. Despite this Jane was a bright child and was chosen to go to a selective secondary school. This singled her out still further as she was offered no financial support either by the education authority or her parents. She wore the same uniform blouse, skirt and cardigan in the sixth form that she had worn on her first day at the school. She stole books for her studies knowing that her parents would refuse to buy them. She was ashamed of herself and left school with no positive sense of identity. She took drugs, dropped out of university and was happy to marry when she became pregnant. She battled to manage the relationship with her small son which had become a reversal of the relationship with her father. She constantly intruded upon him, playing 'kissing all over' games, washing him in a sexualised way and climbing into his bed when her husband was out. At the same time, she loved her son and was unconscious of her need to take revenge on him for her father's abuse. Eventually, Social Services stepped in and prevented her from living with her husband and child. She could not tolerate living on her own and she came into psychotherapy to try and establish a good mother/child relationship. This was partly for the sake of her son and partly to provide her with a 'last chance' to receive good parenting (in reverse). Although this patient benefited greatly from psychotherapy for a number of years, the early damage, including physical damage, was too great. Having worked through threats to her therapist, by bringing knives into sessions, and threats to kill her son if he did not show he loved her, she eventually ended her own life.

Despite making considerable progress in psychotherapy, Jane found it difficult to symbolise. She never stopped hoping that her actual mother would one day be a real mother to her and she did everything to encourage her. One birthday she presented her mother with a beautifully iced cake that she had gone to great trouble to make. Her mother set the cake aside without acknowledgement. She also frequently gave her mother gifts of carefully chosen clothing. Food and clothing were concrete representations of being a good mother and they were what her mother had never given to her. Although a seemingly straightforward gesture, there was another side to these gifts. The clothes were all stolen from a large chain store. When this was talked about in therapy Jane showed considerable anger towards the store, particularly that it flaunted its wares and then expected customers to pay for them. I suggested that the store was the bad corporate mother to whom she had feelings of hatred and revenge that she could not afford to display to her real mother. She felt some guilt over the thefts but the overwhelming feeling was of deep personal shame of being a hopeless, worthless person. Sometimes she would punish herself by cutting herself or putting bleach in her bath water. The physical pain made her feel better.

This patient, who was very disturbed and had had an extremely damaging childhood, never gave up the quest to find a good mother in either her own mother or herself. She employed the defence mechanism of splitting to retain the fantasy of a good mother, as opposed to the bad shop/mother that gave her nothing. In the transference she would quickly swing from experiencing me as one and then the other. She experienced these swings as being in me rather than herself and always had a paranoid eye on me to see when I would turn.

Another aspect of the patient was the way in which her family, comprising herself, her husband and her son, mirrored her family of origin. Whereas she showed a sexual interest in the child of the opposite sex, she called upon her husband to police this relationship and make it safe for her child in a way that her mother had not done for her. The role of the father can be very important in protecting the child from an excess of intimacy with the mother. In the case of a girl the father also has the task of confirming and respecting her sexual development without seducing her by directing her sexual attentions to himself.

Sidoli describes how a patient, attended to in infancy by a mother whose mind is either disturbed or totally preoccupied with personal worries "is forced to use, through lack of maternal reverie, his or her body or bodily organs (instead of the mother's mind) as a container and signifier, as a kind of stage upon which the unfelt psychic pain can be dramatised and eventually relived" (Sidoli 2000: 97). In this extract, Sidoli is writing about psychosomatic patients, but I believe that perversion could be regarded as a type of psychosomatic disorder. The difference is that the perverse patient unconsciously prescribes his or her own remedy for cure. There is not the element of dependency and looking for the dependable other. This is replaced by a defensive system which protects the self against the harm others might impose and is therefore a barrier to change.

Welldon (1988) clearly demonstrated that perversion does not only relate to the sexual instinct but also to the maternal instinct. There is also evidence that other caregivers may compulsively abuse their positions. There have been a number of cases of nurses who have become serial killers of patients. Professor Robert Forrest, forensic toxicologist coined the acronym CASK – Carer Assisted Serial Killing. He calculated that about 1 or 2 per million health-care workers posed this type of risk to their charges.

Dr Harold Shipman, who killed a countless number of his female patients, was one such perverted caregiver. He may not belong in this chapter as he is not a woman, but the 'perverted mothering' he offered to his patients and the relationship with his own mother perhaps qualify him to be mentioned here. "To his patients he was not a killer, he was a marvellous GP, caring, attentive and always prepared to prescribe expensive drugs" (Whittle and Ritchie 2000:320) and again "He gave his victims a gentle, pain-free death, almost as though he was bestowing a blessing" (Whittle and Ritchie 2000:321). At the point of death, he no longer saw them as human beings. He was distanced from them:

they were not real people with families, hopes and fears. He was able to pull down a blind between the old ladies he knew and 'twinkled at' when he chatted to them about their cuts and their aches and pains, and the bodies he dispensed to death. He was able, possibly because of the job he had chosen, to regard those bodies separately from the individuals who inhabited them.

Shipman experienced the slow, painful death of his mother when he was an adolescent. He frequently saw the doctor injecting her with morphine, which temporarily relieved her pain. He could do little to help her, and nothing to cure her or save her from death. He later became a doctor himself and, using morphine, he showed that he then had the control to give his elderly female patients the peaceful, painless death his mother had deserved. (He also killed the patient/mother who had deserted him when he needed her and left him dominated by her for the rest of his life). At his trial the judge summed up the case:

> "Each of your victims was your patient. You murdered each and every one of your victims by a calculated and cold-blooded perversion of your medical skills for your own evil and wicked purposes. I have little doubt that each of your victims smiled and thanked you as she submitted to your deadly ministrations."   (Whittle and Ritchie, 2000, p. 313)

CHAPTER FIVE

Assessment

In psychotherapy it is not always possible to think of assessment as a separate part of the therapeutic process as every session is likely to have some qualities of assessment. This is particularly so when perversion is a prominent feature of the patient's pathology as secrecy, evasion and deceit will be characteristics of the patient's initial communications with the therapist. Perversity as a psychic defence is likely to emerge very slowly in the therapeutic relationship. When looking at the origins of perverse sexuality in early trauma, we are looking back at the parent-child relationship. Emotional, sexual and physical abuse are most often experienced within the family, generally perpetrated by the parent or a close parental figure on the child. It is therefore most important, as with all assessments for psychotherapy that the assessor listens to the patient's account of their infancy and childhood. This would include both that which the patient presents as factual information and the surrounding fantasy material.

It is not my intention to write about assessment per se, but to suggest aspects of assessment particularly relevant to the perverse patient. The psychotherapist should aim to:

1) Detect the operation of a perverse unconscious structure.

2) Assess the extent to which perverse functioning is erotic (sexually exciting).

3) Note the extent of aggression, violence and sadism in the patient's life and in his reported fantasies and dreams.

4) Explore the pervasiveness of perversity and it's dominance within the personality and life-style of the patient.

5) Discover the extent of the patient's awareness of his perverse qualities.

6) Consider the patient's ability and motivation for change through the process of psychotherapy.

I shall now elaborate on each of these six areas of focus:

The Operation of a Perverse Structure

Perversion is a dominating structure within the body/psyche that acts against balanced functioning. Being firmly rooted in body as well as psyche it expresses itself in behaviour as well as thoughts, feelings and fantasies. This means that it interferes at every level and in every aspect of life although, to the patient, it may feel separate and split off from consciousness.

Mr L is a barrister who is looking for therapy because of feelings of desperation around his job and his marriage, both of which he is in danger of losing. He tells the therapist that his colleagues regard him with suspicion because he is known to fraternise within the criminal fraternity. He says that he has a reputation amongst the toughest, hardest criminals not only for representing them very effectively and cleverly but also for "being on their side". He is currently representing such a client who has sacked four previous lawyers and lost his entitlement to legal aid. He tells the assessor, with a twinkle in his eye, that he is sure he will not be financially out of pocket. He also mentions in passing that he is in debt. A female junior colleague has made a complaint of sexual harassment against him that is being formally investigated. He describes a bottom-pinching episode in court that he thinks has been blown up out of all proportion. He says that the woman concerned actually fancies him but won't admit it.

Without knowing anything about this man's history, we have a case that suggests perverse functioning. Mr L is a man with a lot to lose who nevertheless continues to live 'on the edge'. He has a well-paid job, yet persists in behaviour which puts his job and professional reputation at risk. He appears to derive excitement from his association with criminals and is not deterred by the way other people see this. He also hopes to engage the therapist in this excitement by the twinkle in his eye when he suggests, but leaves to the imagination, where the money for his therapy fees might come from. It is only a short jump for the therapist to infer that he is being compromised and might be accused of corruptly obtaining 'dirty money' from the patient. It is typical of such patients to a) catch the psychotherapist out and b) wish to include the psychotherapist in a perverse scenario.

The most general theme to identify in a patient during assessment would be a feeling of compulsion to look for exciting, repetitive short-term solutions to alleviate anxiety. Such solutions would not be steps to an eventual long-term goal, but would militate against genuine satisfaction and eventual self-fulfilment. Examples would be addictive drinking, shopping or playing of computer games (avoiding work). When the perverse tendency is eroticised, this would include the fetishistic use of other people as sexual part-objects. The other person, whether partner or prostitute, is dehumanised with the sexual interest being only in the body or part of the body.

The Extent to which Perverse Qualities are Erotic

There needs to be some exploration of the patient's sexual fantasies. If these are hostile, it will be necessary to assess whether he feels motivated to act on them. Likewise, consideration should be given to non-erotic perverse functioning. Examples of the compulsively deceptive, but apparently non-sexual, perverse personality often appear through the judicial system. Such was the case of the expert forger and antique bookseller, Mark Hofmann. Born into a strict Mormon family, Hofmann began his career as a forger at the age of 14, first by selling forged Mormon coins and later other meticulously produced Mormon documents. One of his most famous forgeries was the 'discovery' of a yet unknown poem by the American poet Emily Dickinson that appeared in a Sotheby's auction catalogue in 1997. Hofmann was an extremely careful worker and the obsessional nature of his perverse personality showed in his attention to accuracy down to the finest details. The paper was correctly reproduced, the hand-writing, which gradually changed during Dickinson's lifetime, was correct to the year of alleged writing, but there was also a personal detail: the addition of the words "Aunt Emily" which Hofmann later said added "a touch of veracity". He described himself as attempting to "read enough of her material until I felt in touch with her muse". The extent to which he did this is evidenced by the fact that he not only forged the document, but also wrote a poem accepted by critics as authentic. He got inside his object. His area of operations might have seemed limited to academic fraud rather than personally aggressive or destructive had he not been cornered and faced with the possibility of exposure. He then showed the force of anger behind his deceit. He made three nail bombs killing one of the people who might have exposed him and the wife of another. He then planned to kill another unrelated person solely to give the police a false lead. Before this happened he injured himself as the third bomb exploded, symbolically attacking his body in the way his perversion was attacking his psyche (Worrall 2000:9-19).

*The Extent of Aggression, Sadism and Violence in Life,
Fantasies and Dreams*

It is often easier to locate the *sexually* perverse themes
within a patient's psyche than the apparently more benign
deceptive qualities in their everyday life. Sometimes the
deception does not seem to be 'embodied'. This was apparently the case of Mark Hofmann, until further investigation
showed that from an early age he was building up a hatred
for the Mormon society in which he lived and this was
centred round the distress of his mother's 'anguish' over his
father's polygamy. It seemed that in the same way that he
had got inside the creative heart of Emily Dickinson, he had
also got inside the broken and humiliated heart of his mother
and taken upon himself her unexpressed search for revenge.
He cheated others in the same way that he experienced his
mother as being cheated. He began by cheating the Mormon
Church. He sold them forged documents which appeared to
undermine the ethical values of their founders, thus causing
them in turn to deceive their followers by keeping secret the
evidence, which they believed to be true. This is an example
of how deception breeds distrust.

Violence is usually a response to feelings of intrusion.
The perverse patient, possibly with a history of sexual
abuse, may experience the intimate relationship of psychotherapy as unbearably intrusive. If the patient is known to
use violence to protect himself, the therapist is placed at risk.
There may also be an increased possibility that the patient
will use violence against himself if he feels abandoned,
misunderstood or isolated from the therapist upon whom
he has come to depend. This may be particularly acute at a
time when he is regressed and is seeking fusion and a loss
of self. Account needs to be taken during the assessment of
any previous attempts at suicide or self-harm. There needs
to be some assessment of dangerousness. The best predictor
of future violence is the occurrence of violence in the past. If
the patient has a history of violence, or gives the impression
that he has problems controlling his violence, it may be pref-

erable to consider group therapy as the treatment of choice. The group would offer a safer container for treatment. If the patient is seen for individual psychotherapy he may need to be seen within an institutional setting where help is readily at hand in an emergency.

The Pervasiveness of Perversity and its Lifestyle Dominance

Direct assessment can be difficult so pervasiveness can often be more easily detected through its opposite. A deceptive person is likely to be adept at deceiving others about his deception. If the patient has no concern about his shadow qualities and also tends to see himself as the object of other people's deceit, this would be a way in. Anyone who goes about presenting himself as squeaky-clean should be regarded with healthy suspicion. As we might be wary of buying goods on the basis of salesman's hype, we might also raise a therapeutic eyebrow at the patient who tries to sell us only the best part of himself. We might suspect that he had something to hide. On the other hand, patients might have learnt in childhood that they *should* hide what they have to show and protect themselves from the threat of unwanted intrusion.

Another, seemingly contradictory sign of the pervasiveness of perverse qualities in the personality structure is the *absence* of erotic feeling in the patient's report of his relationships. Mr N might have been heeding the warning of Philip Larkin when he wrote, "They fuck you up your mum and dad …Get out as early as you can, And don't have any kids yourself" (Larkin 1974:30).

Mr N had been brought up by a violent father and an emotionally cold mother who was a nurse. He could only recall her showing warmth to him when he was ill. He recalled her kissing him only once when she was cutting his hair and accidentally cut his ear causing it to bleed. When he was three years old he was in the kitchen where his two older brothers were boiling a kettle for tea. One of them upset the kettle down Mr N's back causing severe scalding. He was hospitalised for several months during which time he recalls his parents only coming to visit him once. He was told this visit was too upsetting for them to return. On leaving hospital he was sent to a convalescent home and then to relatives abroad with the idea that this would speed his recovery. At the time of coming into therapy, he was living with a girlfriend with whom he very seldom had sex. He could not feel sexually excited about her, which she greatly resented. The couple often used alcohol to blot out their conflicts and feel a sense of togetherness that he could not feel sexually. He felt very angry towards many of the people he encountered in his life. Occasionally he had an outburst of rage in which he would smash something. He once attacked his girlfriend sufficiently violently for her to need medical treatment.

This patient seemed to have recreated his family in the relationship with his partner. To her he was both the violent father and the negligent mother offering no bodily contact or warmth. He held his partner in both hope and despair: feelings he had experienced with his mother. The partnership demonstrated both his own childish impotence and his wish for revenge. Not only was he denying his partner a sexual relationship but he also ensured that she provided for him materially. Unconsciously, he made sure that he earned a little less than he needed to just get by, so that she had to give him 'pocket money' and help to fund his analysis (which he must have felt his mother owed to him). He felt both hopeless and victorious at humiliating his child/partner.

The Patient's Awareness of his own Perverse Qualities

To benefit from psychotherapy, a patient has to be able to share his experience of pain with another person. The assessment needs to explore the patient's capacity to talk about feelings that make him feel badly about himself. It will be particularly useful to know if the patient can describe feelings of humiliation. If the patient can only express his feelings in terms of action and attack on others, he may be difficult to treat. The psychiatrist Bukanovsky, (the Russian 'Cracker'), found that an inability to deal with humiliation was characteristic of serial killers, who become locked into repetitive and compulsive acts of revenge. Serial killers often rape or sexually assault their victims before or after killing them (Kent 1999). As with Dr Shipman in chapter 4, this raises the question of who or what in the inner world is being so insistently killed off by murder in the outer world. Mary Bell's own account of her killing of two small boys when she was herself only a child reveals a confusion or blurring of identity between herself and the victim.

> '"No, no...I'm kneeling in front of him. I think I'm kneeling on a brick. I say.....' She began to cry. "Put your hands around my throat," and he does and ... I put my hands around his throat (her hands are lying open in her lap) and I press, I press, I press ...'
> She had leaned forward until she was bent double, her face down on her knees, her body trembling. She showed no interest in the children as people, the action of killing was what was important."
> (Sereny, 1998, p. 349)

In inner world terms, whom or what was Mary killing? Was it one of her abusive and neglectful parents or was it the unbearable victim part of herself that was conjured up in the younger, more vulnerable child. The latter is suggested by the fascination that Mary had felt after the killing in talking to the dead boy's mother about him, including a request to see him in his coffin.

It is obviously important to listen to how the patient describes his childhood and his parenting. It is also invaluable to hear what the patient has to say about his grandparents and their parenting of his parents. This three-generational assessment not only demonstrates the extent of the patient's insight into the quality of relationship with his parents, but also gives an indication of the model of parenting that his parents might have had in mind, derived from their own early experiences. There is likely to be both deadness and emptiness as well as a push towards frenetic activity in the inner world of the perverse patient. These two opposites may be very apparent as the patient describes himself in the assessment.

The Patient's Ability and Motivation for Change

Consideration needs to be given to the resources of the patient. First of all, are there any physical contraindications to psychotherapy? Fred West, my patient Jane and some of the potential or actual serial killers treated by Bukanovsky had suffered brain damage, either at birth or as the result of an accident or other physical trauma. The extent to which impaired brain functioning will be an obstacle to therapy needs to be considered. Assessment should cover the patient's ability to hold anxiety and to experience the depths of depression rather than divert himself with perverse, anxiety-releasing activities. What defence mechanisms does he use? Does he tend to protect himself through projection? (It is not difficult for a patient to accuse a therapist of strange and bizarre practices). More fundamentally, thought needs to be given to the patient's need for his current defensive structure. It would not be helpful to treat someone who was not able to function once he had begun to disarm himself. Someone who fragments or becomes stuck in total dependency on the therapist would not be well served by engaging in psychotherapy.

Another consideration is whether, as the patient begins to relinquish his defences in treatment, he can be sufficiently contained within the psychotherapeutic setting. If the patient is likely to demonstrate his anxiety and psychic conflict through acting out between sessions, rather than managing to reflect and work through his difficulties with

the psychotherapist, he may damage or destroy the progress
of his treatment. On the other hand, his acting out may be
a useful communication of his psychic state if it can be
subsequently considered in therapy and become a learning
experience that gives shared understanding to the patient
and therapist. In acting out, conflicts within the psychotherapeutic relationship are externalised in the same way
as bodily action is used to address intrapsychic conflicts in
perversion.

CHAPTER SIX

The Psychotherapeutic Relationship

This chapter aims to extend the boundaries of perversion from the psyche and body of the patient, to the relationship between therapist and patient, including the internal world of the psychotherapist.

> "There is no horizon there. There is no continuity between actions; there are no pauses, no paths, no pattern, no past and no future. There is only the clamour of the disparate, fragmentary present. Everywhere there are surprises and sensations, yet nowhere is there any outcome. Nothing flows through: everything interrupts. There is a kind of spatial delirium." (Berger, 1999)

This passage might be describing the chaotic feelings aroused in the treatment of perversion; it is also a description of the Garden of Lost Souls, the dystopian third panel of Hieronymus Bosch's Millennium Triptych.

Perversion glitters repugnantly, fascinating and repelling us, attracting our senses, attacking our memories and challenging our morality. The psychotherapist is caught up in the powerful psychic forces emanating from the perverse patient and is deeply affected by the hostile content of psychosexual fantasy in its variety of heterosexual and homosexual forms. During the onslaught it can become difficult to preserve a solid sense of identity and it may seem that a fiery furnace has replaced the containing alchemical vas. But the angry flames need not be all-consuming. To avoid being overwhelmed the psychotherapist needs to be able to preserve a sense of separateness and a knowledge that the angry sexual whirl in the consulting room is only symbolically incestuous.

Aims

The aims of psychotherapy are two-fold. Firstly, there needs to be a *structural change* in the psyche as the structure in place has a perverse goal. The patient needs to be able to develop and sustain whole-person relationships rather than use people for short-term ends. Secondly, the link between perverse fantasies and compulsive, repetitive action needs to be modified. It is unlikely that perverse fantasies will disappear, but treatment should aim at weakening the power of fantasies to drive the patient into action. The patient then has some sense of choice although this may also bring conflict. The aim of treatment cannot be freedom from conflict. Meltzer (1973) states that the aspiration of psychoanalysis is to free patients from the compulsion to repeat conflicts of the past and eventually, by strengthening the structure of the personality, to allow learning from experience to take place. This is particularly true for the perverse patient who is not at liberty to learn. He has lost his liberty to experience in a new way. He feels and acts as if he already 'knows' and without therapy, fresh experience leaves no mark on his understanding. The aim must therefore be the *management of conflict* through the gradual establishment of a more integrated personality structure that is strong enough to tolerate feelings of being pulled in different directions.

The Therapeutic Alliance and Defences

The psychotherapist has a difficult job in working with the patient towards achieving structural change in the psyche. The patient's psychic structure has to be challenged without his defences being prematurely shattered (a symbolic rape). The first task must be to build a therapeutic alliance. Even this is fraught with difficulty as the patient's perverse psychic structure and resistance to sharing and to reflection militates against establishing a working relationship based on trust. He is likely to have been one of the insecure, avoidant infants in the Ainsworth strange situation test who had learnt not to trust his carer (Chapter 4).

Kalsched (1998) has indicated how the anxiety from overwhelming affect in infancy can be given bodily representation in dreams in such forms as dangerous assailants or ferocious animals. He suggests that "primitive anxiety and its defences are personified in dreams and other imaginal products of the psyche in the form of archetypal daimonic images and motifs. Dreams therefore give us access to early trauma, its affects and defences, in ways not available to us before, and thereby increase our understanding of the 'unthinkable' affects of infancy". He considers that such dream imagery can easily be misinterpreted and is actually the psyche's self-portrait of its own archaic defensive operations. The purpose of such archetypal imagery is to defend against integration; to keep separate the affect connected with early violent experience through fear of re-experiencing it.

Kalsched examines the methods which the psyche adopts to deal with unbearable anxiety associated with a traumatic complex and is in agreement with Jung's assertion that a traumatic complex brings about dissociation of the psyche and forces itself tyrannically upon the conscious mind. This formation of complexes results from the splitting that has been described as one of the characteristics of perversion in the first chapter. Kalsched describes the traumatised patient as having a compulsion to repeat self-defeating behaviour.

He cannot recall trauma in a personal form but only in an archetypal form. It exists in a form that is inaccessible to the ego. The therapist must help the patient to bring the trauma into the world if the system of archetypal defences is to be unlocked (Kalsched 1996:25).

Stein emphasises that the archetypal parent-child situation is reactivated in therapy and some withdrawal of archetypal projections is essential for therapeutic progress to be made (Stein 1973:57). The patient must feel sufficiently protected to allow some of his established defences to be made redundant. The therapist must take some responsibility for ensuring that the witch, wizard, ogre etc in herself does not continue to dominate the patient's transferencial experience of her otherwise the patient will have no choice but to continue to employ every devious device at his disposal to escape from the threat of the therapist's malign supremacy.

Chapter 1 showed the need for the therapist to look at the internal organisation of the patient rather than the level of development. The patient is stuck on a learning plateau unable to move forward and caught in a circular, unprogressive addictive state, driven to relieve overwhelming anxieties through short-term goals, which are destructive to longer-term development. Chasseguet-Smirgel describes a "disavowal of the genital primal scene" (Chasseguet-Smirgel 1985:112). There is an attempt to recreate a primal scene, which is sterile and destined to produce no child. In such a setting there can be little feeling of mutuality or creative partnership. In the patient's transference he is gratifying the therapist: he has become a narcissistic object for the therapist and has lost any reciprocal feeling of the therapist being there for him. Alternatively, the patient may adopt what Fairbairn called a 'moral defence' In this manoeuvre the patient makes himself bad in order to keep the bad parent (therapist) good. This is a defensive and unproductive strategy since it prevents the patient feeling the badness of the therapist and working with this in the transference. The patient has unconsciously rescued the therapist at his own expense and is left feeling ashamed and isolated. He has reversed his own experience of being a part-object by making his therapist less than human (Sutherland 1989:121).

One model of relationship that could be shared with the patient is an understanding that the psychotherapist is working with the part of him that is looking for change against another part that threatens him. This position can be difficult to sustain when times are rough and the patient's defensive splitting and projection forces a reversal of the model. The patient then projects the threatening part of himself into the seemingly untrustworthy psychotherapist. Of course, neither of these positions is static. They are uncompromising reversible polarities between which the patient may oscillate. With each oscillation the therapist is pulled in as a complementary figure, sometimes a victimiser of the patient and sometimes the victimised.

The paranoid feelings in the patient mean that he has a need to get rid of something. At times this may be his anxiety, at other times it may be his sense of badness. Whatever is not wanted is projected onto the psychotherapist who experiences it in the countertransference . The countertransference is the patient's creation (Heimann 1989:77). Alternatively, the psychotherapist may realise that through projective identification she is acting a role forced on her by the patient. The therapist might then want to push back the unacceptable feelings, confirming the patient's fear of his therapist as an angry, retaliatory figure and the therapy as a sadistic attack.

Sandler (1976) introduced the idea of role responsiveness in the countertransference, by which he meant fitting in with the role assigned by the patient (Sandler 1976:61). This concept can be helpful for the therapist who feels unwillingly dragged into playing a part in the patient's perverse scenario. Episodes of the patient's outer life can often be interpreted as re-enactments of an inner world scenario. (This was demonstrated in the case of the burglar in chapter

2). They highlight needs of the patient which have not been merely repressed, but cut off and dissociated. The therapist is faced with the difficult task of achieving a balance between, on the one hand, playing along and being used by the patient in order to understand the scenario, and on the other, making interpretations which challenge the patient's defences and may cause him to retreat.

In the case of the compulsively perverse patient interpretations may have to wait. The therapist may have to hold on to the material for the patient for as long the patient needs to build up trust and to know that he has not repelled the therapist and driven him away.

The patient may have thought-action fusion characteristic of Obsessive Compulsive Disorder in which obsessional thought and forbidden action are experienced as morally equivalent (Rachman 1993:149-154). Unable to think symbolically, the patient experiences having enacted his fantasy, risking shame and humiliation from the psychotherapist.

Another type of fusion originates between the mother and infant:

Mr Y

Mr Y dressed in bizarre, bright, girlish clothes that singled him out for ridicule and attack. He felt an inner compulsion to dress in this way despite looking very unlike his contemporaries. He put his clothes on in a certain order each morning in the way in which he remembered his mother doing when he was a small child and she dressed downstairs. His attire was a mimicry of his mother with whom he had a poor relationship. It seemed that he both got inside his mother's body and humiliated her through gender transgressive clowning.

The Inner Child

The humiliated patient can be experienced as very strong because of the powerful compensatory forces in his inner world and the strength of the transference. The patient might wish to reinforce this illusion of strength in order to protect himself. Schwartz-Salant writes of the need to get away from narcissistic power struggles and attend to the child in the patient, which might be a masochistic child, punishing himself for his own torment. The needs of this inner child are not repressed but split off and dissociated (Schwartz-Salant 1982:159). The psychotherapist needs to get to know this desperate child who has embodied the distress which he cannot bear to re-experience.

Action, Acting and Acting Out

A sexually perverse patient, by definition, expresses his internal state behaviourally, in action and through acting out. Heightened anxiety and tension are associated with activity. Even when the perverse state is not eroticised, the behaviour of the patient (including verbal behaviour) is particularly important, both in and out of the consulting room. The patient is more likely than others to be charming, engaging and wishing to entertain or to please. Beneath this false persona, tricksterish deceptions, lies and fraudulent personal transactions (including monetary transactions) are likely. Personal material may to be elusively communicated through slippery narrative. If the patient is sexually perverse, attempts will be made to eroticise the relationship with the therapist and deflect her from her task.

The perverse patient is likely to *behave* deceptively within the therapy sessions, rather than just talk deceptively. Ford (1995) distinguishes four types of non-verbal deceit. The patient might use any of these in the consulting room either consciously or unconsciously to deceive the therapist:

- Minimisation of emotional expression

- Exaggeration e.g. histrionics or attention-seeking maximization of emotional expression
- Neutralisation i.e. attempting to mask emotional responses
- Substitution of one emotional expression for another e.g. covering feelings by smiling

Interpreting Negative Feelings

With this amount of distorted communication, Rushi Lederman states that empathy and mirroring by the therapist will not be sufficient to help the perverse patient (Lederman 1982:303-321). In fact the patient may feel depressed by finding that he has, either consciously or unconsciously, deceived or duped the therapist. If this happens, it can actually exacerbate internal conflicts rather than work to relieve them. It is necessary that the underlying fear, hostility and hatred be addressed if the patient is to feel that he is seen as a whole. The need to separate from and deny these feelings of lack of identity and self esteem causes some patients to lose their sense of wholeness and to employ defences of denial, splitting and projection to avoid getting to know the parts of themselves which they cannot accept. Redfearn (1985) describes how such processes can function as normal and necessary aspects of the personality rather than symptoms of pathology. One of the main aims of his book 'My Self, My Many Selves' is to illustrate the "migratory nature of the feeling of "I" (p.ix). "This "I" migrates hither and thither to various locations in the total personality, like the spotlight at a theatre picking out first one actor then another" (p.xii). The unconscious aspects of these 'sub-personalities' may appear as more connected with either the personal or the collective unconscious. Redfearn describes sub-personalities as occurring in pairs or in interacting groups. He gives the examples of the mother and infant pair and a witch imprisoning and devouring a child. The relationships between the pairs or groups "unfold according to age-old patterns and according to the personal experiences of the subject, good and bad. The conscious "I" may be in one role at one time, another at another" (Redfearn, 1985, p. 90).

In the case of perverse personality traits, it would seem that the movement between Redfearn's sub-personalities is a very inflexible one. The way the different sub-personalities play out their relationship has become rigid and fixed. It is dominated by past realities and fantasies and blind to the imaginative and creative possibilities of the present (Redfearn 1985).

The Body

Ogden emphasises the importance of the body in the internal communications. He distinguishes three modes of communication with the Self. The first is the *Depressive Mode* in which the person can symbolise and distinguish between symbol and symbolised. The achievement of symbol formation allows one to experience oneself as a person thinking ones thoughts and feeling ones feelings. Thoughts and Feelings are experienced as personal creations which can be understood (and interpreted).

The second is the *Paranoid-Schizoid Mode* in which there is virtually no space between symbol and symbolised – the two are emotionally equivalent. There is a two-dimensionality to experience – everything is as it is. "You can't tell me I don't see what I see." In this mode, thoughts and feelings are not experienced as personal creations but as facts, things-in-themselves, that simply exist. Perception and interpretation are one and the same. Interpretation can be seen as an attempt to twist the facts to distract, to deceive. No need is experienced to mediate between oneself and one's experience.

The third mode is the *Autistic-Contiguous Mode*. This is a primitive psychological organisation operative from birth that generates the most elemental forms of human experience. It is a sensory dominated mode in which the most rudimentary sense of self is built upon the rhythm of sensation particularly the sensations at the skin's surface. The Autistic-Contiguous Mode of experiencing is a pre-symbolic, sensory mode and is therefore extremely difficult to capture in words. Rhythmicity and experience of sensory contiguity contribute to the earliest psychological organisation in this mode. Both are fundamental to a person's earliest relations with objects: the nursing experience and the experience of being held. The relationship to the object in this mode is certainly not a relationship between subjects, as in a depressive mode; nor is it a relationship between objects, as in the Paranoid-Schizoid Mode. Rather it is a relationship of shape to the feeling of enclosure, of beat to the feeling of rhythm, of hardness to the feeling of edgedness. Sequences, symmetries, periodicity, skin-to-skin "molding" are all examples of contiguities that are the ingredients out of which the beginnings of rudimentary self-experience arise (Ogden 1989:11-18,30-45,149).

Communications in the inner world of the perverse patient tend to be predominantly in the Paranoid-Schizoid and Autistic-Contiguous modes. The experience of the body dominates and the demands of the psyche are absolute. There is no room for playful dialogue, for reflection, choice or creativity. It must be one objective of therapy to move towards the patient having inner representations of the outer world which are of the Depressive Mode, implying an ability to stand back, to reflect, to play and not to feel forced into compulsive action.

Deceptive and Perverse Qualities in the Psychotherapist

With any patient the psychotherapist should be expecting deception since she works in a deceptive world. In fact the psychotherapist could be seen as a professional deceiver, inspiring transference in the patient – the patient unconsciously sees her as she is not.

If, as psychotherapists, we are unable to deal with what we encounter, we may need to deceive ourselves through confabulation, simplification and denial. This probably occurs anyway, but may be heightened by fears and defensiveness. Think of the difference between an actual session and how that same session is presented in supervision. The difference might be considerably greater when the patient is perceived as being perverse. The psychotherapist then *tries to make sense* of the patient in the patient's own terms, rather than through the transference/countertransference, because it is often too difficult for the therapist to break through the attraction/repulsion barrier and enter into the intricacies and subtleties of the transference. Rather like hearing that a colleague has embezzled charity funds or beaten his child: we immediately distance ourselves with the idea that it is something we would not do ourselves.

The therapist might find the patient too overpowering and try to abandon him in various ways. One way might be to engage on a superficial level only, which we are often enticed to do by the deceptive charm of the perverse personality. Alternatively, we might split off "the sexual material" from the person himself and deal with it separately on our own. We could deal in this cut off, masturbatory way with our difficulties in relating to both material and patient simultaneously.

If the psychotherapist feels oppressed, victimised or humiliated by the patient, she may then be tempted to retaliate and to use resources that may not appear to be available to the patient. The therapist may employ her knowledge of literature, myth or religion to make eloquent interpretations that do more to impress or seduce the patient than empower him to address his inner conflicts. This perverse use of theory and status is likely to result in the patient becoming both admiring and resentful of the superior knowledge and understanding of the therapist and further away from feeling personally empowered by the therapeutic relationship.

If the therapist has had an abusive childhood, this may strengthen the perverse feelings in the transference. She might experience a re-enactment of her own abuse, or alternatively, might need to protect the patient by being an indulgent mother, determined to give the patient a perfect childhood. Either extreme would obstruct the therapy.

The therapist has become a therapist through working on both sides of a relationship. She is likely to have worked as a patient for a considerable length of time before working as a therapist. As a patient she will have learned to understand her own wounds and the ways in which the structure of her particular personality may both enable her in some respects, but also limit and deprive her. Generally the therapist should be in a position to understand what may feel repugnant, wild or predatory in the patient and resist a need to control or punish him. This understanding will come from a knowledge that her own inner wounds result from the ravages of her internal predators. To be over-judgmental to one's inner predators is to guiltily condemn part of ones self and to ally ones self with the victim part. This suffering of conscience may lead us to feel incensed if the patient seems to be free of any such feelings of guilt about those (inner and outer) whom he has victimised.

If countertransference feelings of being victimised become uncontainable, the therapist may wish to change sides of the victim-perpetrator relationship with the patient and to shame him. The therapist is then trying to victimise the patient. The patient at this point is not receiving treatment but is being given 'a taste of his own medicine'; a taste of the type of experiences that the therapist has to endure. In shaming the patient the therapist becomes untherapeutic. She encourages splits in the patient by splitting herself off from him, retaining her own sanity, health and well being by projecting all the badness in the relationship into the patient. The therapist may make premature interpretations in order to dump the unacceptable back on the patient. It can be difficult to hold and contain the material until a time is reached when the patient is able to reintegrate his projections. The patient might find that the only way of retaining a sense of self worth with such a therapist is through destructive narcissism; admiring his own badness. Such a state is likely to lead to destructive acting out. If the therapist is seen as too perfect (the perfect parent), the patient's only strategy to rival this perfection might be to create himself as parent of the perfect child, or, malignly interpreted, the perpetrator of the perfect crime who leaves the therapist guessing. To address this tendency the therapist needs to re-establish herself as the 'wounded healer' who can acknowledge and treat her own inadequacies by encouraging the patient to do likewise. This should protect the patient from seeing the therapist as a persecutory figure who is intent on diminishing his self-esteem.

Self Respect and Self Management

The patient must be helped to experience himself differently. If the transference is dominated by feelings of persecution, the therapist must help the patient to recognise the interacting persecutor/victim sub-personalities in himself which have come to dominate the other characters in his inner world. If he can recognise the whole relationship within himself, he is less able to fixate on one side or the other. In his inner and outer world he then becomes less threatened and so less threatening. Lambert describes how, if this stage is reached, the patient's gratitude is aroused through having had the experience of non-punitive interpretations in response to the patient's destructiveness. Through knowing and believing in himself, he can begin to trust himself in relation to others and so trust others as they relate to him (Lambert 1981:152-3).

Much of the early work will be addressing the patient's archetypal defences and his identification with the instinctual pole of the archetype. As a balance begins to be restored in the structure of the personality, the patient becomes freer and more able to 'manage' the various parts of himself including his level of self-esteem. Development of internal and external management is supremely important for the perverse patient. Everyone is a risk manager and has to assess internal and external risks and threats. Management techniques have to be installed which reduce the probability of negative events without incurring excessive costs to the structure or paralysing its organisation.

In psychotherapy the self is the manager, the organiser in the inner-outer world and the archetype of meaning. The self establishes patterns that allow the psyche to function in an autonomous and integrated way. Hillman views pattern as another word for soul (Hillman 1997). With this patterning the patient is able to use his emotional and spiritual intelligence to retrieve his humanity.

REFERENCES

American Psychiatric Association: Committee on Nomenclature and Statistics (1994). *Diagnostic and Statistical Manual of Mental Health Disorders (Revised 4th edition).* Washington DC: American Psychiatric Press.

Berger, J. (1999). Welcome to the Abyss. *The Guardian Review,* 20th November 1999.

Beebe, J. (1994). The father's anima as a clinical and as a symbolic problem. *Journal of Analytical Psychology, 29:* 277-287.

Burn, G. (1998). *Happy Like Murderers.* London: Faber and Faber.

Campbell, D., Elliott, C. and Bowcott, O. (1996). A Grim Fantasy That Lead to a Boys Murder. *The Guardian,* 17th May 1996.

Casement, A. (1998). The qualitative leap of faith. In: A. Casement (Ed.), *Post Jungians Today.* London: Routledge.

Chasseguet-Smirgel, J. (1985). *Creativity and Perversion.* London: Free Association Books.

Colton, C. (1825). Lacon. In: R. T. Tripp (compiled), *The International Thesaurus of Quotations.* London: George Allen & Unwin, 1973.

Edinger, E.F. (1994). *The Mystery of the Coniunctio: Alchemical Image of Individuation.* Toronto: Inner City Books.

Fonagy, P. (1991). The capacity for understanding mental states: the reflective self in parent and child and its significance for security of attachment. *Infant Mental Health Journal, 12*: 201-18.

Ford, C.V. (1995). *Lies! Lies! Lies! The Psychology of Deceit.* Washington D.C.: American Psychiatric Press.

Freud, S. (1924). *Remembering, Repeating and Working-through.* S.E., 12. London: Hogarth Press.

Furman, E. (1992). *Toddlers and their Mothers: A Study in Early Personality Development.* Madison, Conn: International University Press.

Glasser, M. (1979). Some aspects of the role of aggression in the perversions. In Rosen, I. (Ed.), *Sexual Deviation* (2nd Edition). Oxford: O.U.P.

Greenacre, P. (1950). General problems of acting out. *Psychoanalytic Quarterly, 19*: 455-467.

Grosz, E. (1995). *Space,Time, and Perversion.* London: Routledge.

Heimann, P. (1989). *About Children and Children – No – Longer.* London: Tavistock & Routledge.

Hillman, J. (1997). *The Soul's Code: In Search of Character and Calling.* London: Bantam Books.

Holmes, J. (1996). *Attachment, Intimacy, Autonomy: Using Attachment Theory in Adult Psychotherapy.* Northvale, New Jersey: Jason Aronson Inc.

Hyman, R. (1989). The psychology of deception. *Annual Review of Psychology, 40*: 133-154.

Johnson, M. (1987). *The Body in the Mind.* Chicago: University of Chicago Press.

Johnson, M. (1988). Self-deception and the nature of the mind. In: B.P. McLaughlin and A. O. Rorty (Eds.), *Perspectives on Self Deception.* London: University of California Press.

Jung, C. G. *The Collected Works (20 volumes)*. (Edited by H. Read, M. Fordham & G Adler, translated by R. F. C. Hull). London: Routledge & Kegan Paul/Princeton University Press.

Jung, C. G. (1916). The Synthetic or Constructive Method, *CW vol. 7*: 121-140.

Jung, C. G. (1936). Psychological Factors Determining Human Behaviour, *CW vol. 8*: 232-262.

Jung, C. G. (1946). The Psychology of the Transference, *CW vol. 16*: 353-466.

Jung, C. G. (1954). On the Psychology of the Trickster Figure, *CW vol. 9 (I)*: 456-488.

Jung, C. G. (1957). Problems of Modern Psychotherapy, *CW vol. 16*: 114-174.

Jung, C. G. (1959). Concerning Rebirth *CW vol. 9 (I)*: 199-258.

Jung, C. G. (1963). *Memories, Dreams, Reflections*, London: Random House.

Jung, C. G. (1967). The Dual Mother, *CW vol. 5*: 464-612.

Jung, C. G. (1969). General Aspects of Dream Psychology, *CW vol. 8*: 443-529.

Kalsched, D.E. (1996). *The Inner World of Trauma: Archetypal Defences of the Personal Spirit*. London: Routledge.

Kalsched, D.E. (1998). Archetypal affect, anxiety and defence in patients who have suffered early trauma. In: A. Casement (Ed.), *Post-Jungians Today. Key Papers in Contemporary Analytical Psychology*. London: Routledge.

Kaplan, L. J. (1991). *Female Perversions*. London: Pandora Press.

Kent, J. (1999). Darkness Visible. *Observer Magazine*, 8th August 1999.

Klein, M. (1975). Mourning and its relation to manic-depressive states. In: *Love, Guilt and Reparation and Other Works 1921-1945*. London: Hogarth Press.

Lambert, K. (1981). *Analysis, Repair and Individuation*. London: Academic Press.

Laplanche, J. & Pontalis, J. B. (1973). *The Language of Psychoanalysis*. London: Hogarth Press.

Larkin, P. (1974) They fuck you up your mum and dad. In: *High Windows*. London: Faber and Faber.

Lederman, R. (1982). Narcissistic disorder and its treatment. *Journal of Analytical Psychology*, 27: 303.

Limentani, A. (1966) A re-evaluation of acting out in relation to working through. *International Journal of Psycho-Analysis*, 47: 274-282

McDougall, J. (1995). *The Many Faces of Eros*. London: Free Association Books.

McLennan, J.D., Lord, C. and Schopler, E. (1993). Sex differences in higher functioning people with autism. *Journal of Autism and Developmental Disorder*, 23: 217-227.

Meltzer, D. (1973). *Sexual States of Mind*. Perthshire, Scotland: The Clunie Press.

Ogden, T.H. (1989). *The Primitive Edge of Experience*. London: Karnac Books.

Ornstein, A. (1995). Erotic passion: a form of addiction. In Scott Dowling (Ed.), *The Psychology and Treatment of Addictive Behaviour*. Madison Conneticut: International Universities Press.

Pert, C.B. (1987). Neuropeptides:The Emotions and Bodymind. *Neotic Sciences Review*, 2: 13-18.

Potter, D. (1993). *Lipstick on Your Collar*. London: Faber & Faber.

Potter, D. (1996). *Karaoke*. London: Faber & Faber.

Rachman, S. (1993). Obsessions, Responsibility and Guilt. *Behaviour Research and Therapy*, 31: 149-154.

Radin, P. (1973). *The Trickster. A Study in American Indian Mythology*. New York: Schocken Books.

Raphael-Leff, J. (1983). Facilitators and regulators: two approaches to mothering. *British Journal Medical Psychology*, 56: 379-90.

Redfearn, J.W.T. (1985). *My Self, My Many Selves*. London: Academic Press.

Rorty, E.O. (1988). The deceptive self: liars, layers and lairs. In: B. P. McLaughlin and A. Oksenberg (Eds.), *Lairs in Perspectives on Self Deception*. London: University of California Press Ltd.

Ross, F. (1998). Pattern. In: I. Allister and C. Hauke (Eds), *Contemporary Jungian Analysis*. London:Routledge.

Sandler, J. (1976). Countertransference and role responsiveness. *International Review of Psycho-analysis*. 3: 43-47.

Schwartz-Salant, N. (1982). *Narcissism and Character Transformation*. Toronto: Inner City Books.

Sereny, G. (1998). *Cries Unheard: The Story of Mary Bell*. London: Macmillan.

Sidoli, M. (2000). *When the Body Speaks: The Archetypes in the Body*. London: Routledge.

Sperry, R. (1986). The new mentalist paradigm and ultimate concern. *Perspectives in Biology and Medicine*. 29: 413-422.

Stein, R. (1973). *Incest and Human Love*. Dallas: Spring Publications.

Steiner, J. (1985). Turning a blind eye: The cover up for Oedipus. *International Review of Psycho-Analysis*. 12: 161.

Stoller, R. (1986). *Perversion: The Erotic Form of Hatred*. London: Maresfield Library .

Stoppard, Tom. (1968). *The Real Inspector Hound*. London: Faber and Faber.

Sutherland, J.D.(1989). *Fairbairn's Journey into the Interior*. London: Free Association Books.

Symington, N. (1993). *Narcissism, A New Theory*. London: Karnac Books.

Warner, M. (1998). *No Go The Bogeyman*. London: Chatto and Windus.

Welldon, E. V. (1988). *Mother, Madonna, Whore: The Idealisation and Denigration of Motherhood*. London: Free Association Books.

Whittle, B. and Ritchie, J. (2000). *Prescription for Murder: The True Story of Mass Murderer Dr Harold Shipman*. London: Warner Books.

Worrall, S. The Impersonation of Emily. *The Guardian*, 8th April 2000.

Wyly, J. (1988). The perversions in analysis. *Journal of Analytical Psychology*, 34: 319-337

Yorkshire Television. *Someone to Watch Over Me*, screened 13th January1999.

De Zulueta, F. (1996). *From Pain to Violence: The Traumatic Roots of Destructiveness*. London: Whurr Publishers.

INDEX

acting out, 8–9, 12, 28, 37, 67–68, 75, 81

addiction/addictive, 9, 11, 14 26, 51, 61, 72

aggression/aggressor/aggressive, 9, 10, 17, 50, 60, 62–63

alchemical
figure, 37
imagery, 14
vas, 70

American Psychiatric Association, 6, 83

anima, 34–36

anxiety/anxieties, 2, 8–11, 13, 15, 26, 47, 49, 61, 67, 71–73, 75

archetype(s), 25, 48
instinctual pole of, 81
of meaning, 82
of the Great Mother, 15
of the Trickster, 3, 34–35, 38

attachment(s), 42–43, 53

Beebe, 36, 83

Berger, J., 69, 83

Bowcott, O., 10, 83

Burn, G., 31, 51, 83

Campbell, D., 10, 83

Casement, A., 37, 83

Chasseguet-Smirgel, J., 9, 12–13, 72, 83

collective unconscious, 15–16, 41, 76

Colton, C., 24, 83

complex(es) 16, 25, 67
core, 9, 15, 29
Oedipus, 49
traumatic, 71

countertransference, 2, 33, 73, 79–80

criminal behaviour/criminality, 11, 28–29
and women, 50

criminal(s), 29–30, 60–61

cycle, 11, 14, 33, 52

defence(s), 8, 13, 16, 24, 26, 40, 55,

59, 67, 71–72, 74, 76, 81 *see also*:
denial and splitting
denial, 12–13, 23, 76, 79
and splitting, 16–17, 76
of difference, 9
De Zulueta, F., 88

Edinger, E. F., 14, 84
ego, 8, 10–11, 13–17, 38, 40, 42–43,
48, 72
Elliott, C., 10, 79
Escher, M. C., 27–28
exhibitionism, 7, 17, 42, 50
extroverted attitude, 11

female perversion, 3, 48, 50
fetishism, 7, 61
transvestic, 7, 17, 49
fixation(s), 9, 11, 23–25, 45
Fonagy, P., 53, 84
Ford, C. V., 20, 75, 84
Freud, S., 3, 11–12, 23, 36–37, 84
frotteurism, 7
Furman, E., 52, 84

Glasser, M., 9, 15, 29, 84
Greenacre, P., 12, 84
Grosz, E., 17, 84

Heimann, P., 73, 84
Hillman, J., 82, 84
Holmes, J., 53, 84
homosexual/homosexuality, 3–4, 70
humiliation, 7, 10, 13, 66, 74
Hyman, R., 84

idealisation, 9, 40
and denigration, 17
incest/incestuous, 15, 19, 41, 51–52,
70
inner world, 11, 17, 19, 20, 22, 36, 43,
66–67, 73, 75, 78, 81

Johnson, M., 23, 43–44, 84
Jung, C. G., 11, 13–14, 16, 22–23, 34,
36–38, 42, 71, 85

Kalsched, D. E., 71–72, 85
Kaplan, L. J., 6, 85
Kent, J., 66, 85
Klein, M., 13, 85

Lambert, K., 81, 85
Laplanche, J., 16–17, 86
Larkin, P., 64, 86
Lederman, R., 76, 86
Limentani, A., 12, 86
Lord, C., 50, 86

masochism/masochistic, 7, 42, 51,
75
McDougall, J., 10, 86
McLennan, J. D., 50, 86
Meltzer, D., 70, 86

narcissism/narcissistic, 15, 17, 30,
38–40, 42, 52, 72, 75, 81

oedipal conflicts, 12, 46, 49
Ogden, T. H., 20, 77–78, 86
opposites, 9–10, 13–14, 34–35, 41, 67
Ornstein, A., 51, 86

paedophilia/paedophilic, 7, 10, 17,
41
paraphilia(s), 6,–7
part object(s), 9, 17, 49, 61, 73
Pert, C. B., 47, 86
Pontalis, J. B., 16–17, 86
Potter, D., 34–35, 86
pre-genital sexuality, 9, 41
psychic conflict(s), 8, 12, 14–15, 47,
67–68

Rachman, S., 74, 86
Radin, P., 34, 36, 38, 86
Raphael-Leff, J., 49, 86
Redfearn, J. W. T., 23, 76–77, 86
repetitive, 24, 51
and compulsive, 2, 61, 66, 70
Ritchie, J., 56–57, 87
Rorty, E. O., 23, 87
Ross, F., 25, 87

sadism/sadistic, 7, 35, 60, 63, 73
sado-masochism, 26, 42
Sandler, J., 73, 87
Schopler, E., 50, 86
Schwartz-Salant, 75, 87
self, 8, 11–12, 14–17, 23, 27, 40, 42,
    56, 63, 76–77, 82
Sereny, G., 66, 87
Sidoli, M., 56, 87
somatisation, 11
Sperry, R., 47, 87
stalking, 8
Stein, R., 48, 72, 87
Steiner, J., 19, 87
Stoller, R., 9–10, 87
Stoppard, T., 24, 87
Sutherland, J. D., 73, 87
symbol(s/)symbolise(s), 14, 22, 25,
    54, 77
symbolic
    house/body, 2
    incest, 15, 70
    activity, 16, 43

expression, 26
rape, 71
Symington, N., 42, 87

transcendent function/link, 14, 26
transference, 43, 55, 72, 75, 78–75,
    79–81
and countertransference, 79
transvestism, 17
trauma(s)/traumatic experiences,
    11, 13–14, 16, 42, 45, 53, 59, 67,
    71–72
Trickster, the, 3, 33–45, 47, 75
triumph/triumphant, 10, 13, 51

voyeur/voyeurism, 7, 10, 17, 51

Warner, M., 87
Welldon, E. V., 48–49, 51, 56, 87
Whittle, B., 56–57, 87
Worrall, S., 62, 88
Wyly, J., 88

Yorkshire Television, 21, 88